WORKac

WORKac

We'll Get There When We Cross That Bridge

Amale Andraos & Dan Wood

The Monacelli Press

Library of Congress Control
Number: 2017939781

ISBN 978-1-58093-499-2

10 9 8 7 6 5 4 3 2 1

Printed in China

Design by Neil Donnelly

Interviews and editing by
Alfie Koetter

The Monacelli Press
6 West 18th Street
New York, NY 10011

www.monacellipress.com

Introduction

We've been working on this book forever.

There was always a more pressing book to write, an urgent research project to launch, an opportunity to engage with another architect's work or to explore what architecture might have been at a different time and in a different place.

But no more excuses. Here it is, just as it is: fifteen years of WORKac.

This book is utterly personal, thus we call it a *duograph* not a monograph: an ongoing conversation between us about architecture, paralleling the conversations we have had about our practice since founding WORKac in 2003—never assuming what architecture "is," but always imagining together what it could become.

While expanding the possibilities to think and practice architecture has always been a given for us, there are a few other principles we discovered as the practice evolved. Some were born out of willful desire and instinct, early attempts to clear new grounds for ourselves. Some were the result of fierce disagreements between us, questions which could only be worked out through the projects themselves—whether research, writing and teaching, or everyday practice. Some emerged in opposition to current trends, authorities, and orthodoxies as well as their assumed necessities for architecture and for architects. Finally, some emerged after everything else was left out—either negated from the start or abandoned after multiple failures. Much was a result of trial and error. None of these precepts has approached something you might consider a stable organizing idea for the office—and yet they continue to inform our work:

First, to commit to our architecture's **engagement with reality**—from the important questions of its time and the strategies of its conception to the contingencies of its context, the specificities of its making, and the opportunities afforded by understanding architecture as lived experience.

Second, to embrace this engagement as **all-inclusive**, bringing together a passion for disciplinary knowledge with curiosity, freshness, and irreverence to add some spice to the myriad of ingredients afforded to architects today. To approach architecture as an open, always-evolving, and yet synthetic discipline is to strive for ways to reinvent it, at once converging lines of inquiry from both within and without.

Third, to design for an **excess of life** against its abstraction: layering legible figures onto and within playful shapes, intensifying textures and colors, multiplying uses and experiences, saturating densities, intensifying lightness, and enlisting humor toward new potential for architectural pleasure across scales, new territories for architecture to exist, and diverse new audiences for architecture to engage.

Fourth, to mobilize this engagement beyond the culturally specific to propose instead that architecture be situated at the **intersection of the urban, the rural, and the natural** as a mediator of projected relationships and material effects that might recast both poles while also reinventing architecture itself, an admittedly utopian attitude that we choose to embrace.

Fifth, to intertwine form and performance in a **narrative of systems and flows**—water, air, light, energy, food—that actively and visibly erode, erase, contaminate, dampen, shape, or perforate what is built and allow for the unbuilt to move through.

Sixth, to **obsess with history** against authority and thus continue to search for alternative models in the past to project new possibilities for the future. To move beyond an assumed common canon and roam instead the many peripheries—and books—in search of otherness's ability to undo centered narratives and expand knowledge. To insist that architecture's most beautiful quality is the fragility of its foundations which demand that the shared ground for its understanding be constantly reconstituted.

Seventh, to maintain a **childlike delight in *making***, set against the fetish of technology through detailed and immediately material physical models that are staged in conversation with the conceptual coherence that drawings enable. Together they form an endless capacity to prototype and mock-up ideas.

Eighth, to embrace **design through disagreement** as a process: to never agree to disagree but rather to continue to disagree until we agree, holding difference together to produce something *other*. To agree to disagree is to agree to start over.

Ninth, to **hold together opposing ideas**: our postmodern critical education, aesthetic sensibility, and professional genealogy together with our love for the promise of modernity in terms of its ideals, positions, and the architectural engagements— from objects to cities—that it inspired. But also, our belonging to a "generation" that would never consider itself as such.

And so, this book is a collection of projects organized along two overlapping yet independent structures. The first structure is rendered through the idea of "five-year plans" as a scale of time through which to construct a practice, but also retrospectively reflect on its often accidental evolution. In the first five-year plan (2003–2008), the practice focused on interiors and the stories they can tell beyond their particular circumstances. The second five-year plan (2008–2013) negated architecture in favor of the urban, finding within the questions around the natural, the rural, the ecological, and the infrastructural significantly more inspiration than within the problem of the bounded formal object. With the third five-year plan (2013–2018) a return to architecture as the collapse of interior and urban scales onto the scale of the building, with a renewed intensification of a building's boundary as site of architectural focus, invention, and imagination—at once thickened and porous.

The second structure consists of ten projects and ten issues through which a set of other works and ideas are engaged. These "lenses" constitute the various ingredients we have dialed up at different times to explore particular approaches and interests, at times architectural and at other times borrowed from outside disciplinary specificity. While not perfectly chronological, these frames do register an evolution in the practice's focus and sites of investigation.

A student once commented at a lecture that our work was like a tasting menu. While this didn't sound great at the time, it now feels like a productive way to engage this book and the past fifteen years: as a series of in-depth investments into questions explored through architecture and design, and which together constitute a shared experience and the beginnings of a body of work. The body's parts are not held together by those questions and frames but by the projects themselves, which are never answers but rather always an attempt to open up new questions about architecture for us— its limits, its potential territories, and its future possibilities.

—Amale Andraos

WorKac Rules

2003

1. ACT BIGGER
2. STAY GLOBAL
3. THE INSIDE IS DIFFERENT THAN THE OUTSIDE
4. PLANTS, ARE IMPORTANT & ANIMALS
5. WHEN IN DOUBT, PAINT IT BLUE

2003— (post-dot-com bubble)

Say Yes to Everything

2008

We leave OMA and the enormity of the global projects and master plans we were working on. No more Business Class travel. We start the office in our apartment: the living room is the workspace, the dining nook is our model shop, and the kitchen counter holds the printers and fax machine. Late nights, the office moves into the hallways for cutting large boards and spray painting in the emergency stairs.

We wait for the phone to ring. Our first project is a doghouse. Being good urbanists, we design Villa Pup—a doghouse for the urban dog—with three video screens, a treadmill, and an odor machine, allowing the city dog to experience the life of its rural cousins. From there we commit to saying "yes to everything"—from bathroom renovations to zoning analyses. By the time we launch an exhibition as part of the first New York New Practices award in 2007, we have more than a hundred projects to show. Someone asks us to teach: Dan at Cooper, Amale at Harvard. We say yes to that. In 2005 we both start teaching at Princeton. Despite our commitment to "work" as a means to discover our voice, we have become academics almost by accident, by not saying no to anything. Diane von Furstenberg is on a yacht in the Mediterranean and

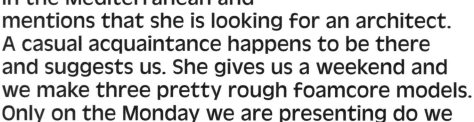

mentions that she is looking for an architect. A casual acquaintance happens to be there and suggests us. She gives us a weekend and we make three pretty rough foamcore models. Only on the Monday we are presenting do we

realize we have come late to the party, at the tail end of a months-long architectural competition. She likes one idea, the "shaft of light," and we win the project. The shaft becomes the "stairdelier" and DVF Studio Headquarters, completed in 2007, is our biggest built project for many years to come. Our teaching at Princeton on ecological urbanism leads to an in-house summer research project on urban plans. The result is *49 Cities*— a study that re-presents visionary urban projects through an "ecological lens," stripping them of their sociopolitcal or economical baggage to focus on how they perform in terms of density, FAR, greenspace, and infrastructure. Each plan is redrawn and color coded to include the systems beyond the cities' limits, our first foray into connecting the urban, the rural, and the natural. In turn, *49 Cities* leads us to our design for the annual MoMA/PS1 Young Architects Program competition, which we win in the beginning of 2008.

In 2007, we had been selected for the NYC Department of Design and Construction's Design Excellence program and in 2008 we were given the opportunity to design a new branch library for Kew Gardens Hills. We start the design, amazed and grateful to be building the most public of public buildings in our own city.

In 2017, it is still under construction.

Dan X Wood
White Street is proof that architecture can help create new ways of living. Ten years later our clients Lela and Brandon are still living there, hosting amazing events for friends and in support of their philanthropy.

Amale Andraos
White Street indulges in stories and an embrace of narrative. It's Soane-ian.

DX   There is no generic in the project; everything is specific.

AA   It's an upside-down triplex in Tribeca: the ground floor, half the basement and a third of the sub-basement.

DX   We created density through difference and varied experiences through programmatic and material stripes.

AA   It is an enfilade that alternates between expansion and compression. The living room holds a chandelier-table that drops from the ceiling. The dining room is surrounded by a thickened frame of storage. Its floor lifts up in parts to become a table.

DX   We thought they'd use the Japanese-style seating maybe once a year, but they eat there all the time.

AA   The stainless steel kitchen is followed by the felt media room. In the corner is the cousins' sleepover loft.

DX   The apartment is 100-feet long, so in the absence of natural light, we created a 40-foot high void in the middle with a staircase connecting all the levels.

AA   Their little dog, Stitch, was getting older and couldn't climb stairs, so Stitch got his own elevator, shaped like a doghouse.

DX   We call that the "Stitchevator."

AA   The back of the apartment is a townhouse-like stack of bedrooms on three levels. The kids' bedrooms end in a series of skylit bridges, with two "homework tubes" on either side of their shower. Between, light is allowed down to the rooms and courtyard below.

DX   The master bedroom has a secret tunnel across the void that connects their shared closet to her mega back-closet.

AA   There are multiple intertwined circulations: the stair, the kids' loft; the dog's elevator; the shortcut through the closet. Upstairs, all the tables connect across the sequence of rooms, creating a dining table long enough to accommodate 70 people. It can also be used as a catwalk.

DX   At one point construction was being held up by the developer, we were all pretty upset. We said, "You know, the sub-basement is only used for building storage . . ." Brandon and Lela said, "Let's make a tequila nook." So we stole some space. When that door closes, time stops. What happens in the tequila room stays in the tequila room.

AA   This is our excess project.

Tribeca, New York

White Street Loft

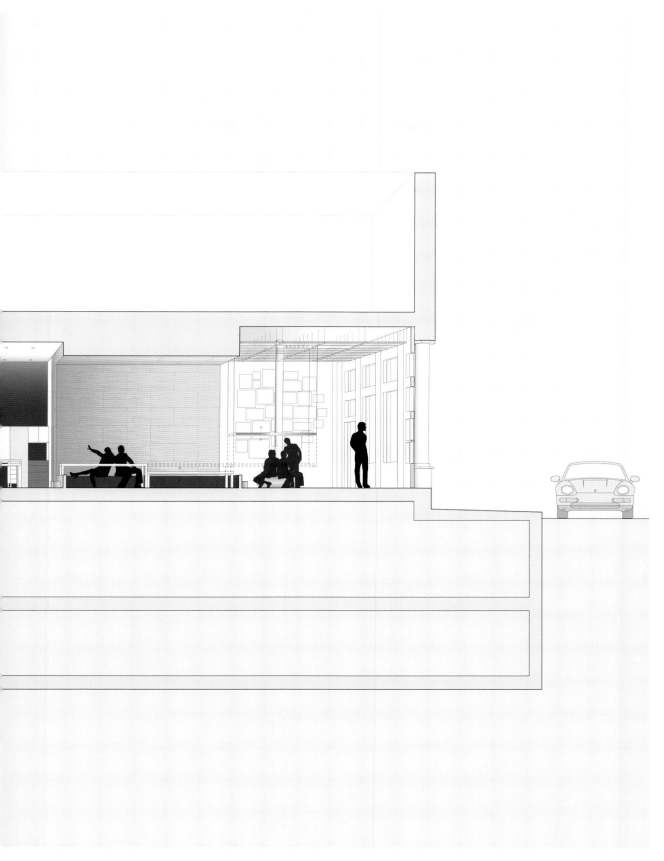

White Street Loft

Tribeca, New York

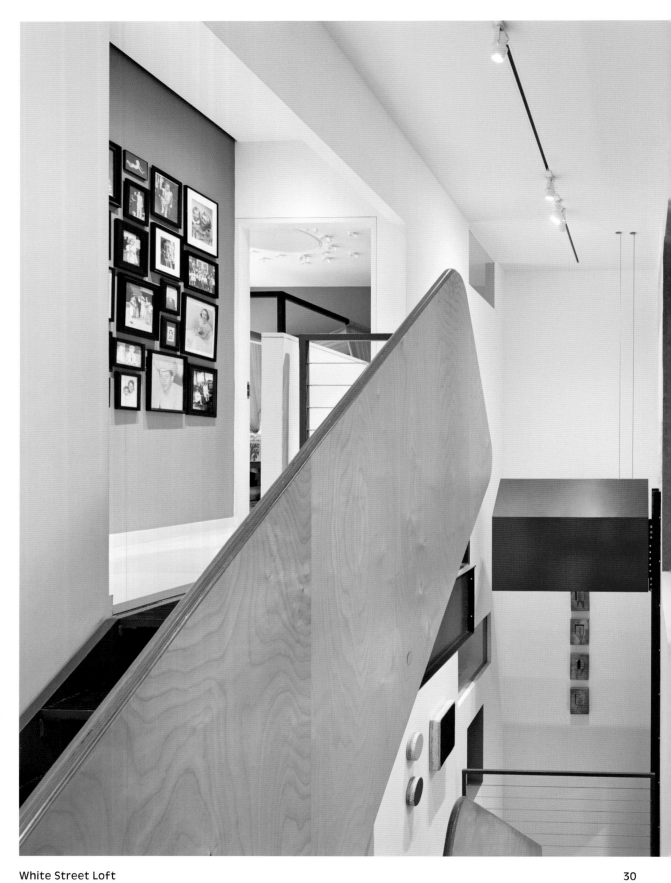

White Street Loft

Tribeca, New York

White Street Loft

Tribeca, New York

White Street Loft

Tribeca, New York

Inner Life

<u>AA</u> It took a while to adjust to the scale of work that was available to us when we first started in New York. We had come from working in Europe, where we were involved in very large projects. Over there, it is common for emerging practices to start with master plans and work through urban issues. That's how they launch their offices.

In New York, on the other hand, young practices are working at a very small scale doing kitchen or bathroom renovations, or in our case with Villa Pup, a dog house! It is immediately very intimate.

37

<u>DX</u> Very intimate, with very small budgets, short schedules and—luckily—no lack of ambition. I think that all added up to our focusing on the diagram as a way to maximize a strong conceptual approach. We weren't going to maximize anything with time, or money, since we didn't have any to work with.

<u>AA</u> The diagram allowed us to bring a number of larger issues to bear on smaller projects, applying strategies that you would use for a building or a city plan but compressing them to the scale of an interior. I have always loved Emilio Ambasz's 1972 show at MoMA, *Italy: The New Domestic Landscape*, in which ideas about cities intersected with domesticity, objects, and landscapes. There is something liberating about treating these interiors as environments: fields to be charged in different ways.

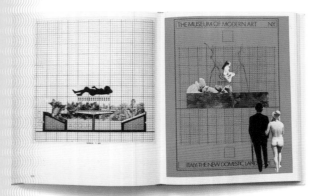

<u>DX</u> Many of the strategies we developed added a certain amount of complexity to the interior experience by challenging expected relationships between inside and outside. They weren't *just* interiors, but the interiors often themselves contained other interiors so that we were creating "outsides" on the inside. Even the freestanding dressing room at Target was creating a space within the space just by closing a curtain around yourself.

<u>AA</u> My favorite diagram from those early projects is the *wiggle*.

That started as a concept for a gym called *Pure Form* and then became the organizing strategy for our exhibition design for *The Good Life*. The wiggle multiplies spaces and experiences and deals with ideas of compression and density in both plan and section within even the smallest possible interior.

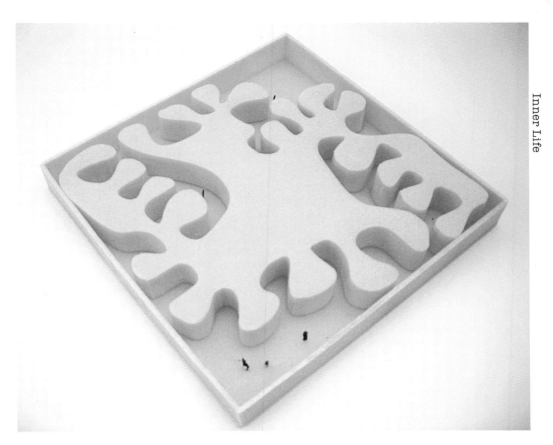

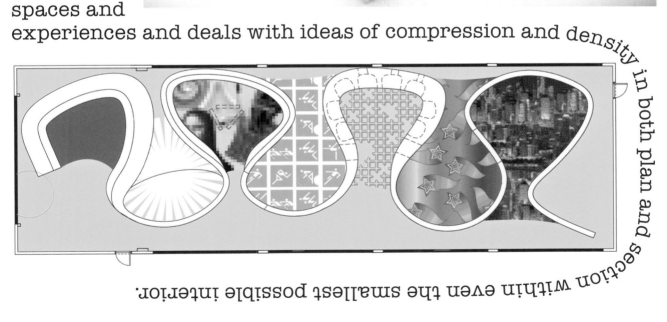

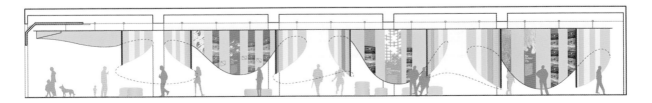

the
connected
city

the
24-h
city

<u>DX</u> There's a Möbius strip-like quality to it, disrupting your sense of being either inside or outside of something, and creating dueling realities depending on which side of the wiggle you find yourself on.

<u>AA</u>   The onion skin was another early diagram, where a central program—like the tasting room for the catering company Creative Edge—is wrapped in layers of other ancillary programs, or circulation.

<u>DX</u>   The D'Amelio Terras Gallery surrounded the main gallery with the entrance, a project room, archives, and offices.

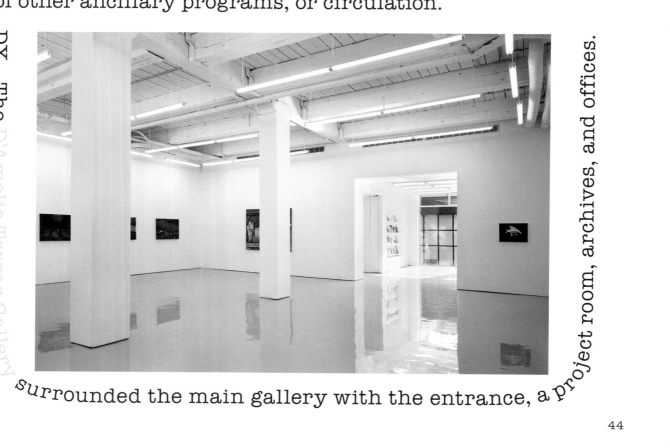

Spotwelders is also a classic onion scheme, with the IT room in the middle serving four editing suites which are themselves used to configure a series of more private lounges around the perimeter of the building.

<u>AA</u>   Maybe because of our focus on the diagram we never fetishized the detail in the way that many New York firms do. A project like the first Children's Museum of the Arts was all about creating different spaces, experiences, and impact through color, scale, sequence, and spatial relations, but not through materials or details. In retrospect I think we have become more attuned to the intricacies of detailing, but early on

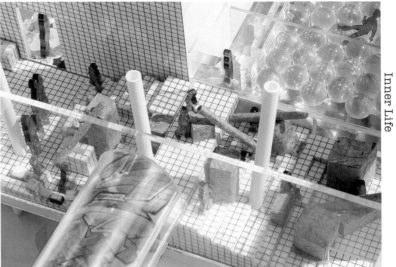

DX Our work from that period was very graphic. Not tectonic at all. We engaged with narrative and program and texture and color and mass and density. Maybe because we designed a stage set for Big Love at the Dallas Theater Center as one of our first projects, we were more interested in the story.

it was like, "What do you mean, how do you turn a corner? You just turn it!"

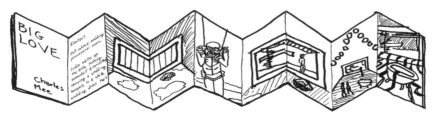

Those early projects with Creative Time—the Information Hub and the Media Outpost were certainly about material investigations, but using car jacks, spray foam, hay bales, and sunflowers rather than more typical architectural materials. It might also be because we started with commercial projects rather than residential ones.

AA   Sometimes, as for the jewelry designer Lee Angel, we used the company's products as a kind of detail—in that case the beads. We weren't into typical architectural details, but there were things that we just became obsessed with: the organization of ceilings, lighting, the thickness and distance between shelves, the heights of hang bars. Working on Prada, we knew certain retail rules by heart.

DX   And then our clients broke them! The Prada rule was to leave four inches between hangers. When we did Target they put four hangers per inch! It was a sixteen-to-one ratio, so our support detail couldn't handle the load and everything started to sag.

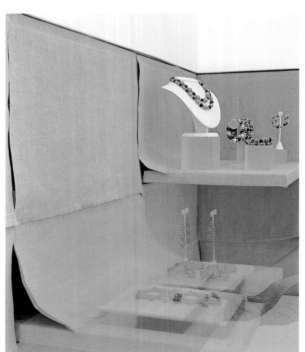

AA   The Creative Time offices were a good jump into detail.

DX   And into materials! From the felt "cones of silence" for the offices to the resin floor and colored glass sliding doors. From starting out with having no material samples in

the office, that whole project became a first material exploration in a way.

AA   A real palette. You used to say that interiors are like short stories that we're writing on the side while working on a novel. I don't know if we have gotten to the novel yet, but we have definitely cranked out the short stories, from the Good Life which completely transformed an unused pier into public space to the minimal and aqua-blue Stoga Stair. Interiors were a way to start our own inner life of ideas.

DX   That embrace of the richness of materials, the creation of a diversity of spaces, and the focus on the clarity of concept continues to inform the way we work now. We never forget the importance of the interior. Even with our models, material reality comes into play very early on.

AA   Interiors are usually what you end a project with, but we start with them.

Anthropologie

AA   Right as we were hitting our stride with the interior projects, and beginning to explore ideas about nature and cities, we also were completing a new store for Anthropologie.

DX   Anthropologie had been very successful and saw that other brands were starting to copy them. They wanted to experiment with a new store design and were open to change.

AA   They already had a very strong identity. We did a three-month research phase into their brand and discovered a "natural" sensibility that paralleled our own interests. This allowed us to start pushing outside-inside relationships and the carving of "no-shopping" relief zones within the store.

DX   That research came to fruition when we built the Dos Lagos store, in the Inland Empire.

AA   The site represented what you don't want to see happen: endless sprawl and an outdoor "lifestyle mall" in the middle of nowhere.

DX   It was called "Dos Lagos" but when we got there, there were no *lagos*. There was nothing but a complete artificiality.

AA   To be intimately engaged with an exurban project was a little disturbing. We were inspired by the fact that the site had been a field of orange trees. Much of the thinking about the rural and the natural was unconsciously making its way into our work.

DX   The perimeter of rooms and atmospheres is really an extension of White Street's excess, but it's the site and context that inspired the cut with the orange tree and the crenellated facade with its areas for sitting in the shade. Those interventions created non-shopping outdoor spaces.

Dos Lagos, Corona, California

Anthropologie

Dos Lagos, Corona, California

Dos Lagos, Corona, California

Anthropologie

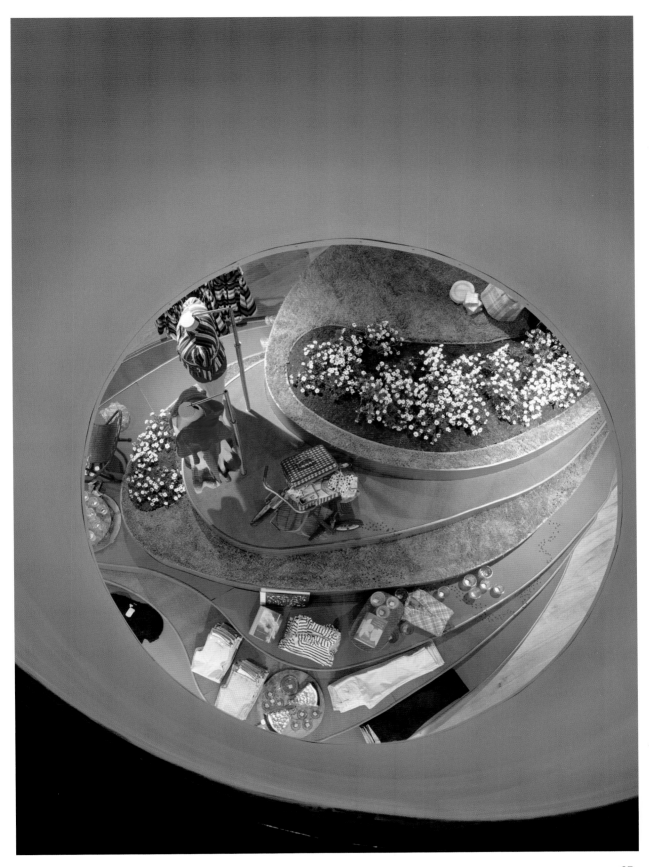

Dos Lagos, Corona, California

Anthropologie

Dos Lagos, Corona, California

Context

<u>DX</u>   *Context* is a complicated word. There is always a context within which you need to define context. Context today means something different than it did thirty years ago, for instance.

<u>AA</u>   Absolutely. Its meaning is always shifting relative to larger social, cultural, and economic forces. I think our

own idea of context started to develop with the Anthropologie project, and then to take on a very lived meaning when we were in Ordos, in the Mongolian desert. There, we really began to understand the

larger condition of global practice in architecture and to realize that there is always a context, even in the "middle of nowhere." Sometimes that context is global practice itself.

DX   We were invited, along with ninety-nine other architects, to be part of building a new residential district, in what

became one of the best-known Chinese "ghost cities," forty kilometers from the existing city of Ordos. Each of us were given standard lots to design houses. The lots were defined by

Ai Wei Wei and Herzog & de Meuron, equally spread in a large

terrain and connected by curving roads. When we visited the site we found these lot lines spray-painted on the sand. And that was it. That was our boundary. That lot was the space allocated to our thinking as architects.

AA   There was never an opportunity to challenge the suburban model put forth by the developer. There was the possibility for a more utopian way of imagining the site—it was literally a tabula rasa—but the point from which we were all starting was so non-utopian.

DX   There were many interesting conversations that came out of this, though. About what context meant to each of the architects involved, because the site was so empty and

devoid of obvious reference. Was the context the discipline? Was it some idea of a Chinese or Mongolian vernacular? Was it about reconnecting with an authentic or traditional mode of building? A lot of teams picked up on Ai Wei Wei's black brick buildings in Beijing, for example as a kind of authenticity.

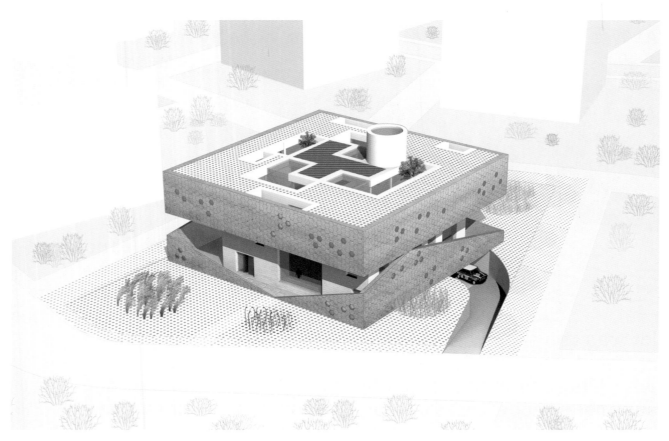

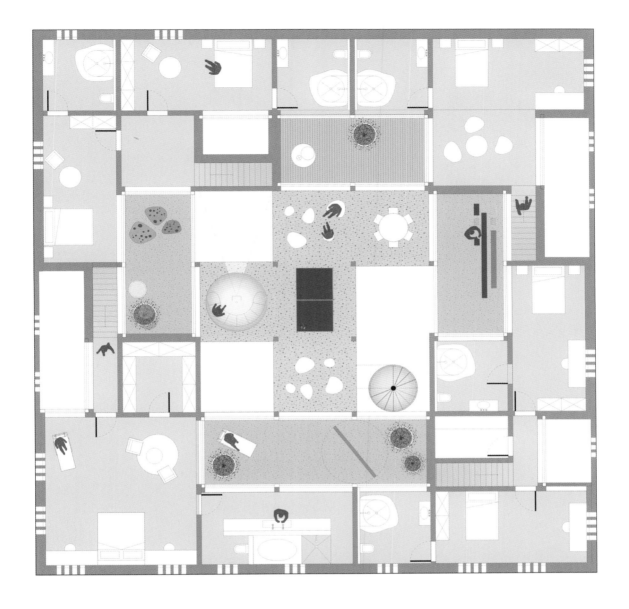

<u>AA</u>   I think we resist that romanticization of craft or authenticity.

<u>DX</u>   We are suspicious about notions of cultural difference or specificity because the overwhelming tendency is for architects to narrow things down to the least interesting reading of a culture. If you bring in questions of identity to architecture it becomes very exclusionary.

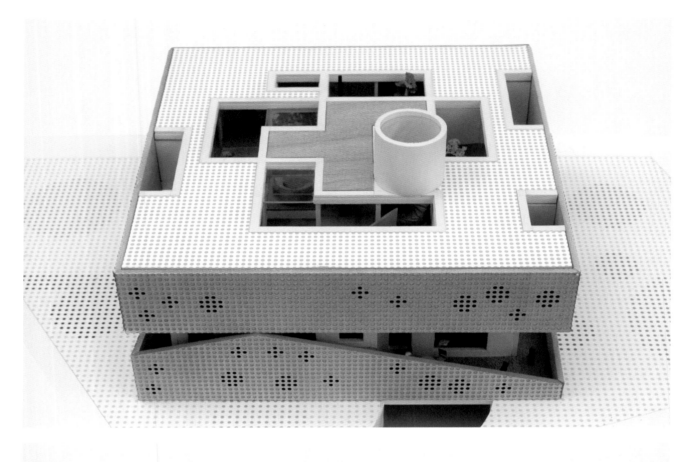

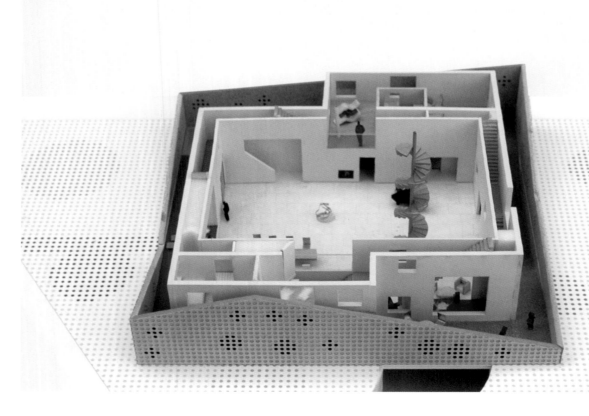

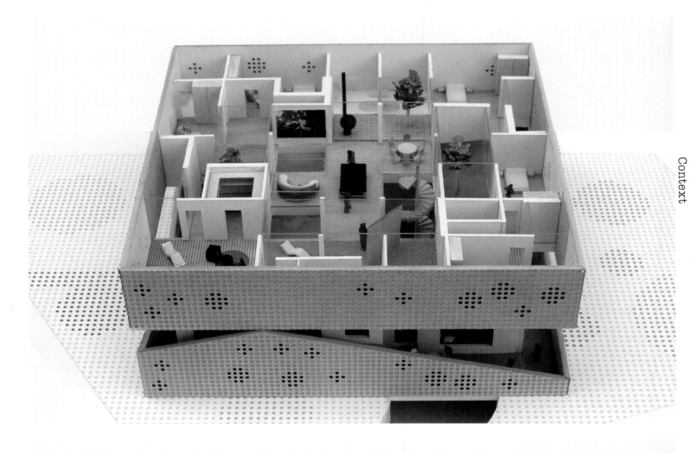

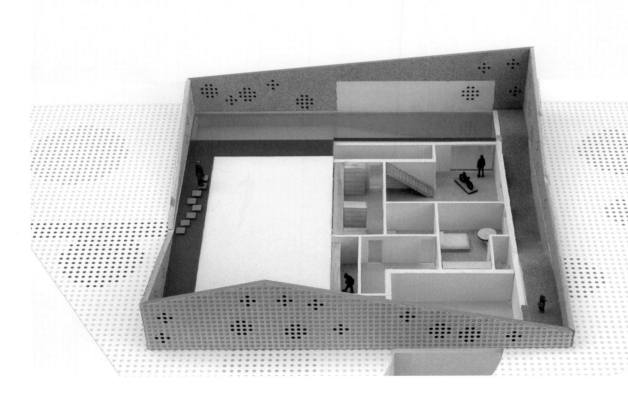

<u>AA</u>   We have a real desire to move beyond questions of identity. Today context is something that is literally burning.

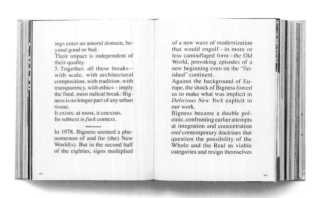

ings enter an amoral domain, beyond good or bad.
Their impact is independent of their quality.
5. Together, all these breaks—with scale, with architectural composition, with tradition, with transparency, with ethics—imply the final, most radical break: Bigness is no longer part of any urban tissue.
It exists; at most, it coexists.
Its subtext is *fuck* context.

In 1978, Bigness seemed a phenomenon of and for (the) New World(s). But in the second half of the eighties, signs multiplied

of a new wave of modernization that would engulf—in more or less camouflaged form—the Old World, provoking episodes of a new beginning even on the "finished" continent.
Against the background of Europe, the shock of Bigness forced us to make what was implicit in *Delirious New York* explicit in our work.
Bigness became a double polemic, confronting earlier attempts at integration and concentration *and* contemporary doctrines that question the possibility of the Whole and the Real as viable categories and resign themselves

You can't just say, "fuck context" as Rem did because today that would mean "fuck the planet." It's not just "fuck history" or "fuck the past." Ordos was the moment where we started to zoom out from the idea of context as limited to the built environment and started to think about the term more broadly. There is never "nothing." There is always an environmental context to work with.

<u>DX</u>   We first thought about this in Bocas Del Toro, Panama, where we were designing a small residential building. It was a strange situation where the mayor had decided that context meant a certain colonial type of building from the time the region was an enormous banana plantation. As long as what

you designed looked like that type of building, it didn't matter if it was covered in vinyl siding, if it dumped sewage directly into the lagoon, or if it was massively enlarged. There, in a place branding itself as an ecotourism destination, they were only interested in context in terms of historical typology, whereas it seemed to us more interesting to look at it in environmental terms.

<u>AA</u>   The environment as context provides a certain amount of consistency across sites and scales, whether they are in Ordos, Bocas, New York, or Dos Lagos. In this sense, I think we are quite contextual. Looking at our generation of architects, who were starting practices around the 2000s, it seems that a number of the most interesting practices have emerged quite locally, meaning they are embedded in the condition of the city they have been practicing in for a long time. You look at the architects who were invited to the Ordos 100 project. Bow Wow is Tokyo. Office KGDVS is

Brussels. Minsuk Cho is Korea. Johnston Marklee is LA. It's a very networked and expanded set of friendships, conversations, and exchanges, and architecture culture is supposed to be more global than ever, but everyone is actually pretty local.

DX But we're always being dumped into different situations, different contexts. Even next door, we can be involved in an industry or a place we don't know anything about. One of the great values of architects is our ability to bring an outsider's eye to whatever situation we are in, to more clearly see it and represent it back to our clients. We allow them to see their world in a different light.

AA Part of operating in the global context is that you

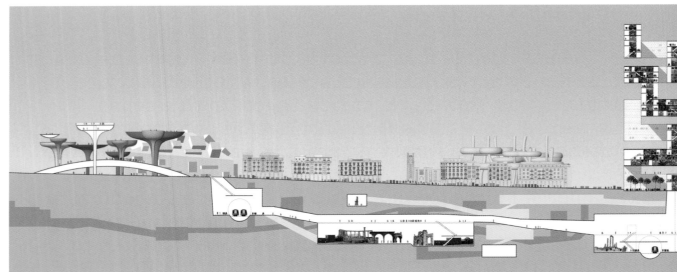

are always
thinking and
practicing
relationally.
That was
one of the
central ideas
of our Cadavre
Exquisse
Lebanese
proposal for
downtown
Beirut, that
we could
create new
institutions
around shared
programs and
situations
rather than
as markers of
identity: music
performances,

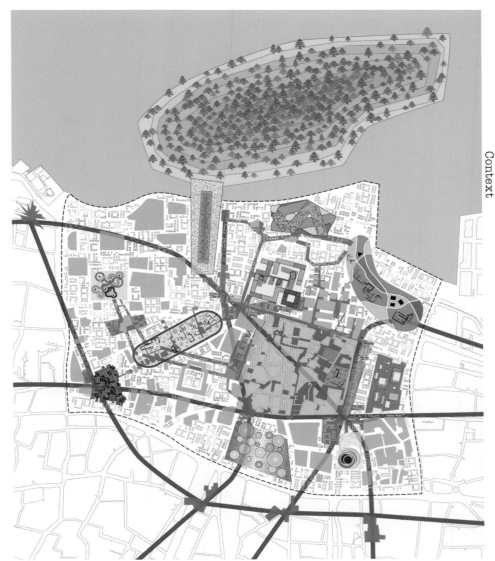

secular education, food, the Mediterranean climate.

DX The environment has that potential to be universal. It is not exclusionary in the way that identity is and has often enabled critiques of the architectural canon. That is what has been interesting for us: to enlist *environment* and its multiple meanings as a robust ground for our own explorations.

DX   The only requirements for the Young Architects MoMA/PS1 competition were to provide water, seating, and shade for parties. By 2008, after years of fab-lab canopies, we thought the annual competition needed to be shaken up.

AA   We landed in New York in 2002 and felt very much like outsiders in the sense of not being interested in the parametric, the leftovers of the formal discourse, or fabrication. Instead, our interests in ecology and urbanism were growing.

DX   In 2008, we had just finished the urban research for our book *49 Cities* and we both read Michael Pollan's *The Omnivore's Dilemma*.

AA   The book brought together cities, farm, food, and everyday life; it connects what is on your plate to the whole world.

DX   We set out to marry this new interest in food systems with the types of urban infrastructures we had been looking at in *49 Cities* to see if we could build a piece of a visionary city.

AA   Forty years after May 1968's famous Parisian slogan "Underneath the pavement, the beach!" we proposed "Above the pavement, the farm!" and called it PF1, Public Farm 1.

DX   A completely off-grid, biodegradable, and recyclable cardboard-tube farm—with the party infrastructure below.

AA   I think at one point we had 150 people working on it—a network of people who would not have come together otherwise. Farmers, chefs, artists, architecture students, and GreenTeam farmers who were graduates from the GreenHouse program on Rikers Island run by the Horticultural Society of New York.

DX   And soil scientists.

AA   PF1 is about inserting architecture somewhere it doesn't belong. To declare that it could actually do all of these things. It set us on a new trajectory.

DX   It is our first project with such a clear agenda, outside of its external parameters and contingencies.

Long Island City, Queens, New York

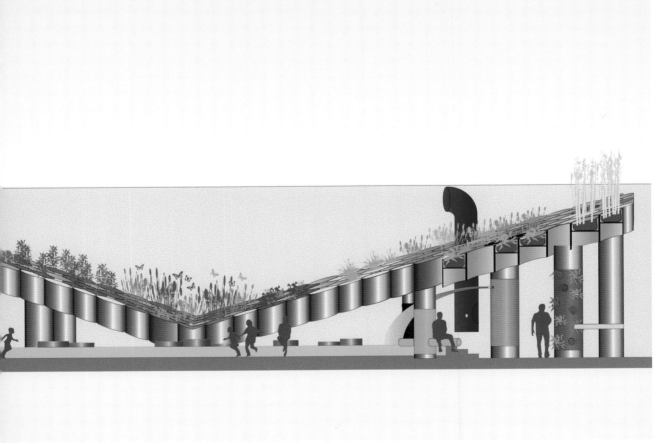

Long Island City, Queens, New York

Long Island City, Queens, New York

Long Island City, Queens, New York

Long Island City, Queens, New York

Long Island City, Queens, New York

Infoodstructure

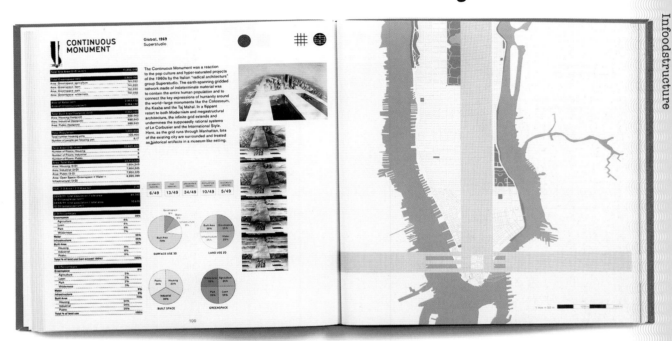

DX   PF1 started off as almost an academic exercise: let's build Superstudio's Continuous Monument and put a farm in it. At the beginning it was such an abstract idea. Farm was just a four-letter word on a page. It just meant green space, a pattern. . . .

AA   . . . and by the end it became a whole world. What *49 Cities* brought forward was that while these visionary cities had been extensively analyzed from the perspective of politics, ideology, or their social context, no one had looked in detail at their shades of green: how they engaged with open space, with parks and forests but also with systems

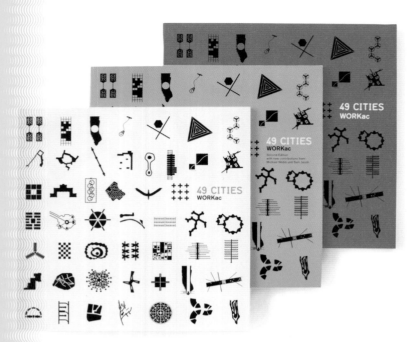

of farming and food economics.

DX   It's not that the future of food is to grow it in cities, but that engaging food systems opened up a different and more holistic way to talk about infrastructure. Embracing systems and food was simply the catalyst that allowed us to open up our thinking.

AA   At the same time, you could say that our interests in these infrastructural systems—whether through urbanism or ecology—were increasingly woven together and brought into architecture. Architecture's boundaries became porous, not by blurring the skin, but literally, by collecting water from the roof and drawing it into the building, for example. Architecture became a medium to organize all of these systems and ideas as part of a larger infrastructure and ecosystem, which connected it back to its context.

DX   At the time a lot of people were asking us if we were looking at the work of Dickson Despommier, who designs

vertical farms that are completely interiorized in power-sucking, multistory buildings that are embedded in an urban landscape.

AA   Our network was farmers, eager to produce food in new ways. In contrast, Despommier's propositions

102

prioritized engineering over farming. And while our position is certainly guilty of being nostalgic for a more rustic era, reading Michael Pollan made us quite critical of that kind of technological superfluity.

DX We made a counter-proposal, Locavore Fantasia. Going

vertical can be about more than engineering food to grow indoors:

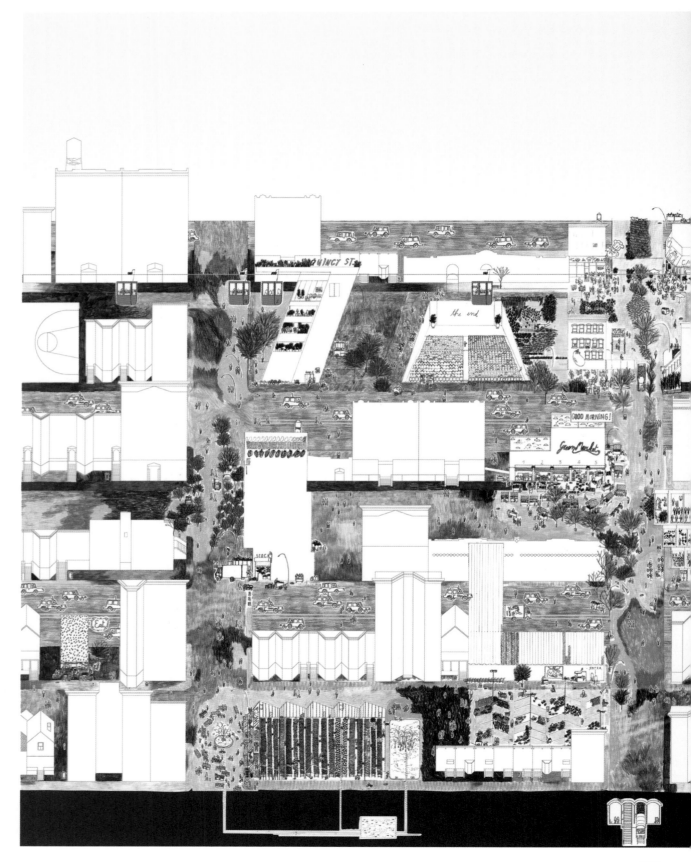

you can design for in-soil growing, have every farming floor open to the sun, and rather than isolate the farm from the city, make the farm a part of it.

<u>AA</u>   It's actually only doubling the ground once, that's an achievable level of urban density. Think of community gardens or rooftops. Infoodstructure was a similar idea—what would happen if streets were turned into farms, assuming fewer driverless cars. It was about transforming what is already there rather than putting faith into a new kind of skyscraper.

<u>DX</u>   We were interested in how people

were developing new ideas about farming, at a time when architecture seemed to have exhausted itself. That led to a fascination with aquaponics: a system where fish, plants, and water are combined in a continuous loop of cleaning, growing, and eating. You can use the same water over and over again. That loop for us had incredible formal possibilities. A lot of our inspiration was—

<u>AA</u> —making the loop visible! That became our Aqualoop

project—fish and plants combined with a sushi restaurant and a playground. The systems are generative of the architecture. You take the lines of the

system and at some point you thicken them.

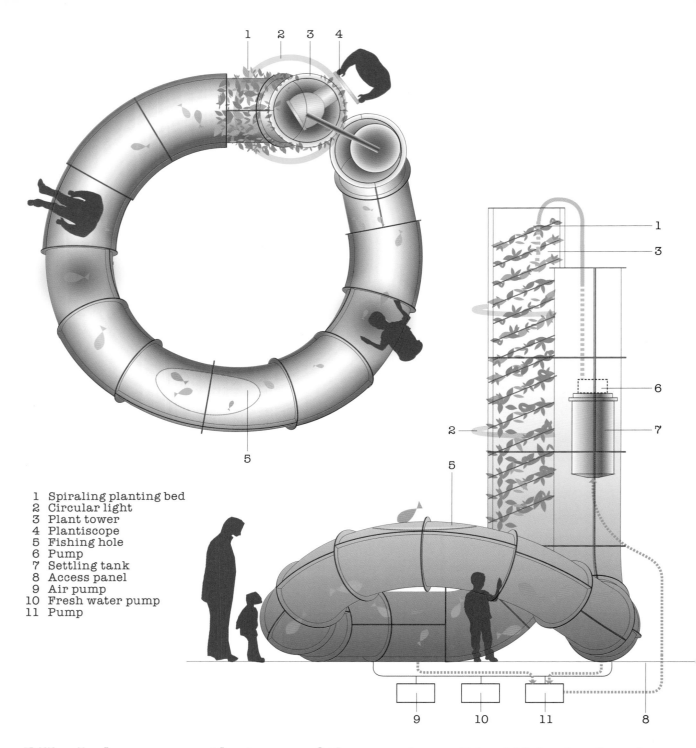

1 Spiraling planting bed
2 Circular light
3 Plant tower
4 Plantiscope
5 Fishing hole
6 Pump
7 Settling tank
8 Access panel
9 Air pump
10 Fresh water pump
11 Pump

<u>DX</u> I always say that one of the most exciting things about architecture is that someone's floor is another person's ceiling. There are these relationships that translate through the section, whether it's transforming the Guggenheim into a lazy river and hydroponics tower for the Flow Show

FLOW
SHOW

gio!

or enlarging a typical core to contain new ecological infrastructure and public spaces as we did for the Plug Out project. In embracing all of these systems it becomes so clear. A sloped roof collects water naturally, and it is collected in a cistern, which becomes a curved wall. The section becomes a system in itself.

<u>AA</u> Soon after we won PS1 we had an interesting conversation with Winy Maas of MVRDV, who had also been looking at food systems and cities, especially with their—

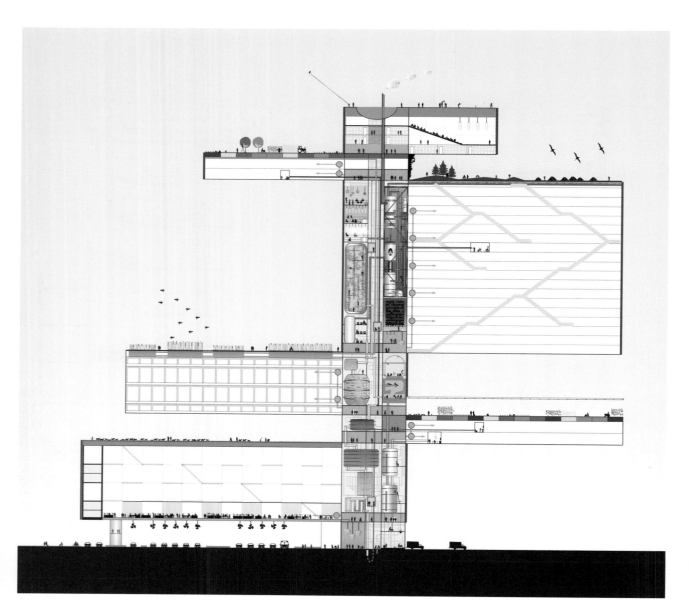

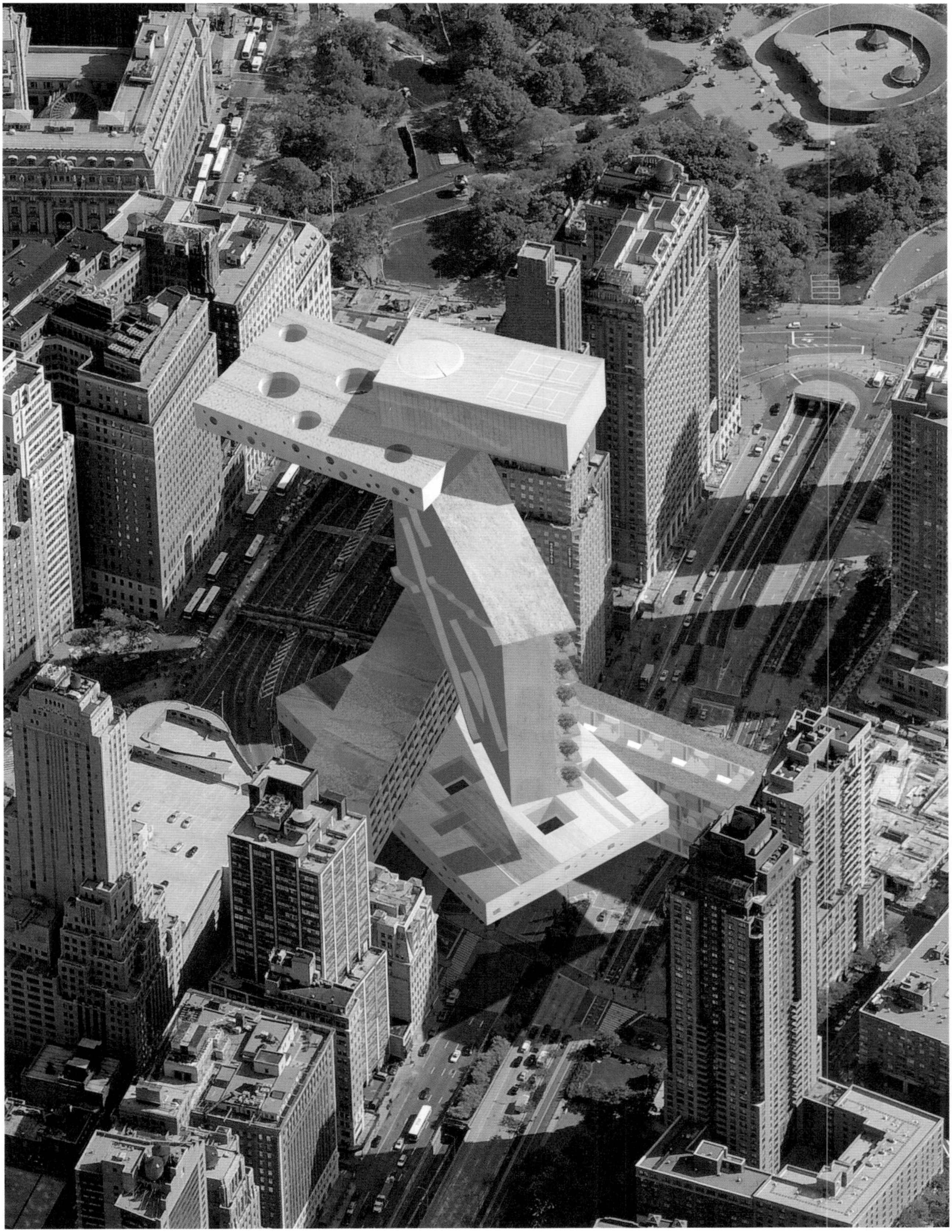

<u>DX</u>   —Pig City—

<u>AA</u>   but the conversation made us feel somewhat more American, and less in tune with that kind of Dutch engineering, pragmatism, and the stacking of pigs. Maybe we're more romantic or dangerously nostalgic.

<u>DX</u>   But our pigs would be much happier.

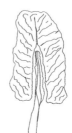

2008–

Make No Medium-Sized Plans

2013

(post-housing bubble)

Urban
farmers

Tired of fab labs, 3D milling machines, parametrics, and everything virtual, we decide to focus our PS1 pavilion design on the most real thing we can imagine—food. PF1 (Public Farm 1) celebrates visionary urbanism, urban farming, sustainable infrastructure, pleasure, color, and engagement. Involving more than 150 people, we establish a completely new network of collaborators, from chefs to farmers, scientists, artists, activists, Rikers Island GreenHouse program graduates, and solar-panel installers trained in off-grid technology in Alaska. Having moved our office to Ludlow Street in 2007, our office mates, the graphic design firm Project Projects, are frequent collaborators and contribute greatly to PF1. We are driven to complete everything we had described in our initial proposal, including furniture, blender stations for vegetable cocktails, a flag, picking skirts, tee shirts—Total Design on steroids. We design PF1 in January, it is selected in March, opens in June, and remains under constant maintenance and harvesting through November. 2008 is all about PF1, and we end the year hundreds of thousands of dollars in arrears—just in time

A model of the proposal by Work Architecture that won this year's Young Architects Program at the P.S. 1 Contemporary Arts Center in Long Island City, Queens.

Betting a Farm Would Work as a Design Project in Queens

Dan Wood and Amale Andraos with elements of their design, which includes growing heads of lettuce and harvesting them.

115

for the crash. In December, we agree to sell our copyright interest in the design of the Diane von Furstenberg stores, after completing twenty-five in a dozen countries in a year. The windfall allows us to pay off our debts and we start the recession at zero. Despite the bleak outlook, we use the recession to our advantage. As work dries up, we embark on a series of speculative projects, working through new ideas about nature, cities, and infrastructure. We look at feeding New York

WORK BC

CLARK EXHIBITION
CANCELLED 12/16/08

2009

within a 100-mile radius by moving everyone in New Jersey into Newark. We propose eliminating streets in the food deserts of Brooklyn and putting up "infoodstructure" instead. We design fish farms and vertical farms and expand our design research into food systems, and pick up with Edible Schoolyard NYC where PF1 left off. We go all-out in our embrace of infrastructure and systems, combining large-scale thinking with continuing small-scale building in New York. Make No Medium-Sized Plans is our mantra. We propose a number of eco-urban master plans in China. One of these, a competition for the redesign of Hua Qiang Bay Road in Shenzhen which connects four new subway lines with public infrastructure, is awarded to us and we momentarily think we are

saved and on our way. This is the project that will launch us. Three years later with no contract and most design elements eliminated by the city, we hand it off to our local partners who complete it years later. We finish two books, *49 Cities* and *Above the Pavement, the Farm!*—an oral history of PF1. Our daughter Ayah is born in 2010. In 2012 we are invited for a competition in Gabon and design L'Assemblée Radieuse, a conference hall for the African Union that is a once-in-a-lifetime invitation to coalesce our ideas about nature and cities, infrastructure and design, representation and global practice, into one uniquely complex building. We win the competition. Our son Kamil is born soon after. Suddenly it seems like a happy recession.

119

In 2011, the Kew Gardens Hills Library officially starts construction with politicians and gold shovels.

Edible Schoolyard NYC
at P.S. 216 & P.S. 7

Gravesend,
Brooklyn, New York
2009–13

East Harlem,
New York
2012–16

AA   We fell in love with this project from the first moment: To build the first Edible Schoolyard in New York! A greenhouse and kitchen-classroom that would introduce kids to issues of food and cities.

DX   The original Edible Schoolyard is in Berkeley, so the first question became one of translation. How do we do in cold urban Brooklyn what they were doing in sunny open Berkeley?

AA   NYC is not a favorable climate for growing food year-round, so the greenhouse took on a more important role. It was also about density—creating a compact structure that allowed for a larger garden. The building comprises three programs that are expressed as their own physical parts. There is the blue rubber "systems wall," the "decorated shed" of the kitchen classroom in the middle, and the greenhouse. Each is distinct, but they all work together as a single building.

DX   We enlisted everything we had learned from PF1: how to collect rainwater, how to create an edible garden, how to use solar power and integrate different systems. We also wanted to think of the project as a new typology. The building is institutional in that it belongs to the school, but it also isn't in other ways; it works on the residential scale without being residential. It's a negotiation between the two.

AA   Ultimately it was important that this project be part of a larger school with its own curriculum and pedagogical agenda, and so the building introduced a new complementary agenda, itself becoming a learning tool.

DX   It was designed to engage a kid's sense of curiosity, to get kids to think about the way the building, its systems, and surrounding garden worked together, and through that to reconsider their own relationship to the environment.

Gravesend, Brooklyn, New York

Edible Schoolyard at P.S. 216

Gravesend, Brooklyn, New York

Edible Schoolyard at P.S. 216

Gravesend, Brooklyn, New York

133

Edible Schoolyard at P.S. 7

East Harlem, New York

Pop

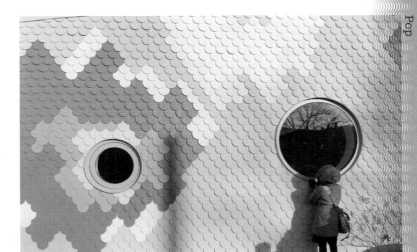

DX What is "Pop" for us?

AA Well, the Edible Schoolyard NYC flower pattern is a very direct reference to Venturi and Scott Brown's Best Showroom—both a pop reference in itself, and part of a lineage of pop appropriation.

DX And in that project we really had to fight for aesthetics. Is there something about a pop sensibility that makes it more difficult for people to accept?

AA No, I think architects always have to fight for the aesthetic quality of their work. You can say that architecture is about drawing a line, literally, in terms of design and aesthetic considerations but also in terms of the projects you take, how you engage them, and to what extent you compromise. If you don't draw that line you aren't doing architecture anymore, which is why aesthetics is a fight worth taking on.

DX One way we draw that line is in color. Our use of loud, poppy colors becomes one of those things we have to argue for and many clients are afraid to use too much color. In our own apartment, for example, we really let loose.

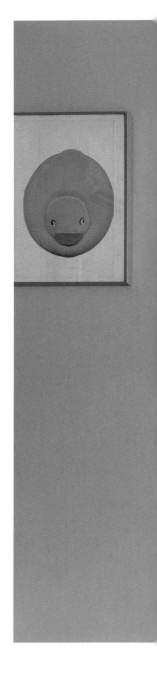

AA It isn't always so difficult. When we designed the Fifth Avenue Apartment, we had a client who said, "I hate pastel and if you are going to use color it has to be bold."

For the Children's Museum of the Arts, they were very focused on art education, so the colors became a color wheel

of every possible shade; it created a fun zone for the kids in contrast with the neutral art studios—while also performing pedagogically.

We also share that as a personal sensibility: the drawings you and I do have always been colorful and that has influenced our architecture, somehow. I know very much where that comes from for me: my father, who is a painter. Color was always fundamental to him, together with ideas about

Pop

composition and noncomposition. I grew up adoring Memphis and Gaetano Pesce and all of this whacko decorative art.

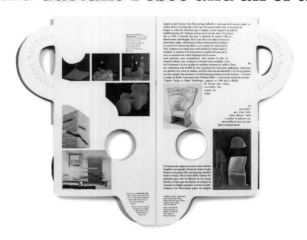

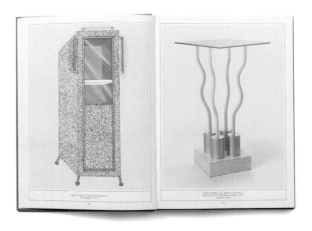

DX For me, not having an architectural background maybe had an impact. I studied film and art history. Gaetano Pesce was big for me, too. I was the only person at Columbia

interested in Pesce and then my studio critic invited him to our final review, especially for me. And he came!

So pop is a lightness, a playfulness and an embrace of color. But, like we always say about humor in general, it can be used—like a joke at the beginning of a serious speech—to disarm people and make them take a look at something differently.

<u>AA</u> Right. We've often been asked why the work is "so happy." Obviously pop is not necessarily happy. Its full of contradictions: it's at once childlike, immediate, and quite complex. It is also an aesthetic sensibility that is very strategic. It is loud—and that loudness has been used as effective political commentary, for example.

It can also be cheap, providing maximum impact for minimum investment. Our Spotwelders project was very pop.

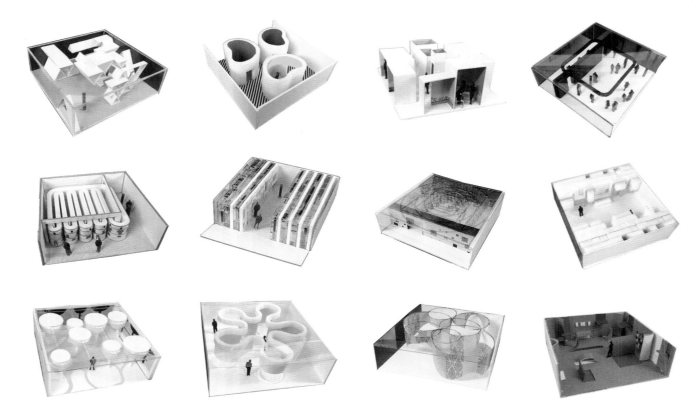

We went for the cheapest possible carpet and radically customized it just by editing out colors. Pop is also about legibility, and it speaks to our love of simple shapes that get complex through certain operations but don't shy away from remaining clear figures. That happened in our project for Kate Spade, for example, where circles in plan are combined to create odd spaces. For the

Edible Schoolyard NYC systems wall at P.S. 216, each element—

toolshed, cistern, composting area, HVAC, and bathroom—has its own expressed

Pop

<u>DX</u>   Pop is also a way to broadcast, to attract as large of an audience as possible, to broaden architecture's public. The materials we use are sometimes pop in that way. In our proposal for Creative Time in Miami, we used sand—the beach itself—to create spaces for people to gather in.

We used Play-Doh to model Wild West Side, our Hudson Boulevard proposal, as a way to immediately communicate a certain sensibility through a material and colors that everyone is familiar with and can relate to.

AA   It's about—and I think here of Warhol, Lichtenstein, or Oldenburg—taking something that is very generic and transforming its material, its meaning, its context, its scale in an effort to defamiliarize it. To go back to the Venturi Scott Brown pattern for Edible Schoolyard NYC, we added to the original set of appropriations and transformations: an interior wallpaper, blown up in scale to become an exterior metal-clad facade, was now losing its resolution as a new copy, rendered in overscaled pixels made of cheap cement-based exterior shingles.

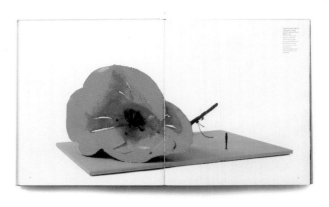

DX   It was taken from the wallpaper they had in their house. I think this is important because part of what we like about pop is that it is transgressive in terms of the personal and the collective, the interior and the exterior.

AA   It confuses the boundaries between what is architecture and what is paint.

POP-ARCHITECTURE
POPPAS

LEFT TO RIGHT:

CURTIS SCHREIER
+ CHIP LORD
(ANT FARM)

GAETANO PESCE

JAMES WINES
(SITE)

AA   If there was ever going to be a visionary rethinking of suburbia you could imagine it happening in Oregon.

DX   And that's what we wanted to do for the MoMA *Foreclosed* exhibition. We wanted to rethink the suburbs in a way that made them both more urban and closer to nature. It was a question of simultaneity. How can we have both at the same time?

AA   It was also asking what the minimum "essence" of urban density could be, and how artificial and constructed "nature" could get. With these two things in mind we developed our scheme: a grid of piers defined by two streets with swaths of open green space running in between.

DX   We were very careful about the proportion of the blocks and the distance between the two streets. We wanted to make sure both wildlife and a rich diversity of plants could exist. We had to figure out what the minimum dimension would be for that to happen.

AA   While what was in between the piers was close to untended, the housing blocks were more landscaped, and developed as ecological infrastructures. Each block became integrated with a certain system—whether for composting organic food or collecting and recycling water—which informed the design of various new housing typologies.

DX   We were emphasizing an idea of community through infrastructure where each house is part of a system that makes the entire city work together. No one housing type stood on its own. If one housing block processed heat, then the steam would go to another housing type that would use it to generate power and another block would distribute it.

AA   It is a very symbiotic proposition. Maybe someone will actually build it.

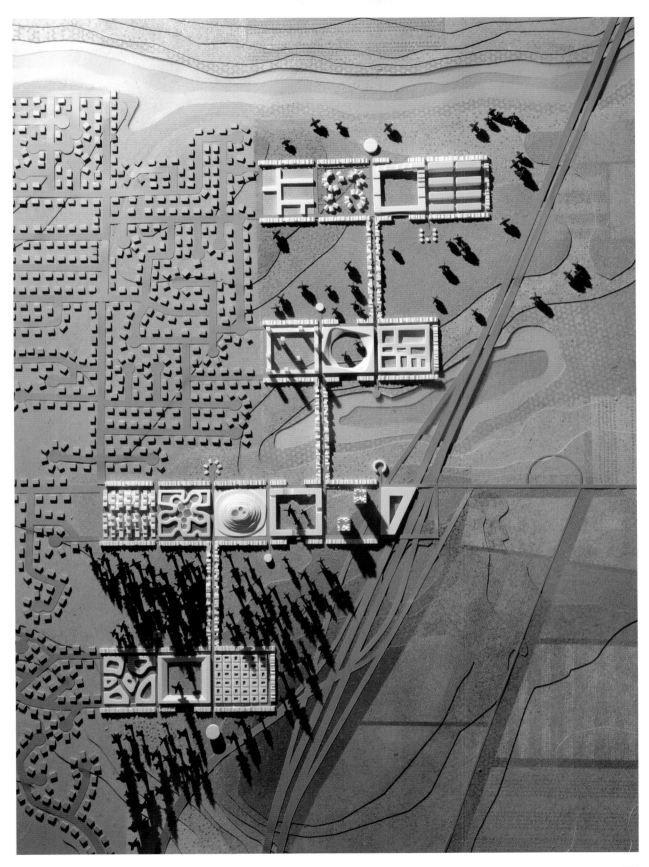

Keizer, Oregon

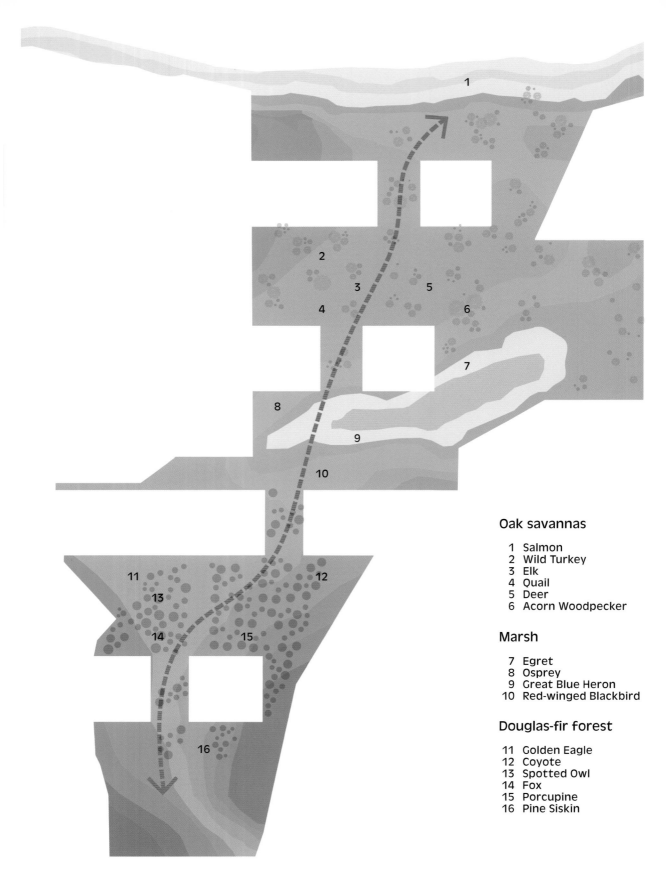

Oak savannas

1 Salmon
2 Wild Turkey
3 Elk
4 Quail
5 Deer
6 Acorn Woodpecker

Marsh

7 Egret
8 Osprey
9 Great Blue Heron
10 Red-winged Blackbird

Douglas-fir forest

11 Golden Eagle
12 Coyote
13 Spotted Owl
14 Fox
15 Porcupine
16 Pine Siskin

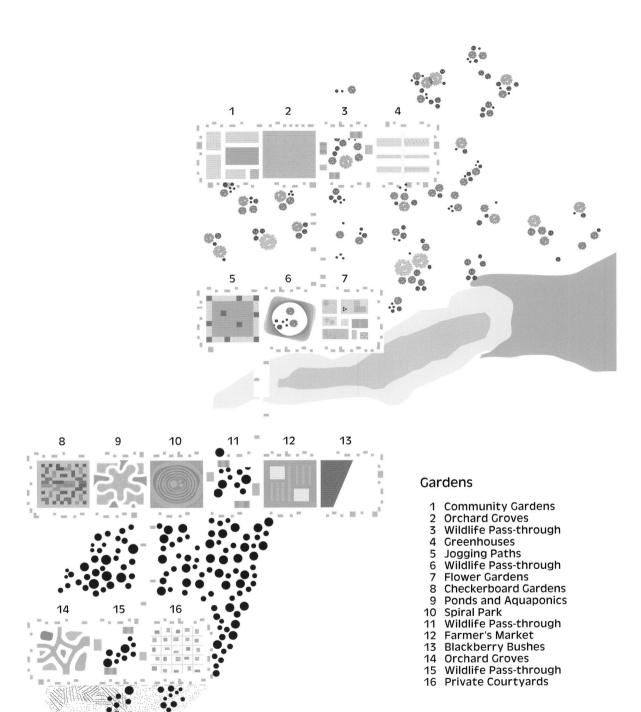

Gardens

1 Community Gardens
2 Orchard Groves
3 Wildlife Pass-through
4 Greenhouses
5 Jogging Paths
6 Wildlife Pass-through
7 Flower Gardens
8 Checkerboard Gardens
9 Ponds and Aquaponics
10 Spiral Park
11 Wildlife Pass-through
12 Farmer's Market
13 Blackberry Bushes
14 Orchard Groves
15 Wildlife Pass-through
16 Private Courtyards

Nature-City

Keizer, Oregon

Keizer, Oregon

Nature-City

Keizer, Oregon

Urbanism

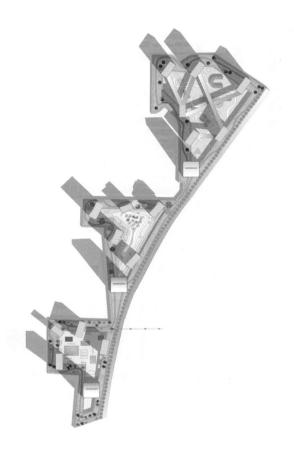

<u>DX</u> Green Belt City
was our earliest urban
project. We never show it
anymore, but it already
has all of the elements of
Nature City in their most
primitive form. The project is based on the requirement
for a 15,000-space, aboveground parking garage for a huge
residential development. In Las Vegas no one was ever going
to park on the roof, which created the possibility for a public
park. The green space mitigated the highway and the parking
and filtered wastewater for irrigation. There were three
courtyards, just like L'Assemblée Radieuse in Gabon, each
one with a different landscape—with parking piled around the
outside to make an elevated walkway.

<u>AA</u> There, the natural and the urban integrated through
systems, but also through section, which is an idea that

carries through our work. In Green Belt City, an elevated highline looks down on courtyards and hides the parking. In Nature City the section allows for the east-west grid of urbanization to be cut by the north-south grid of nature as it weaves through and under the buildings.

DX   It would be great to draw a sectional version of *49 Cities*. It is easier to compare all of those cities through plan, but in some cases that just doesn't tell the whole story. Radiant City, for instance, has more than 100 percent green space because there are gardens on the roofs and under the buildings, which are raised on pilotis.

AA   *49 Cities* is a never-ending project for us: When we started the research it was incredible to realize how many architects were addressing issues of urbanism and the city, especially in the '50s, '60s, and '70s.

DX   Every single architect would design a city, basically as soon as they graduated from school. We asked Michael Webb of Archigram, "Why did you guys design cities?"

AA   And he said, "That's just what we did! We had our day jobs and then we designed cities at night." Now, architects

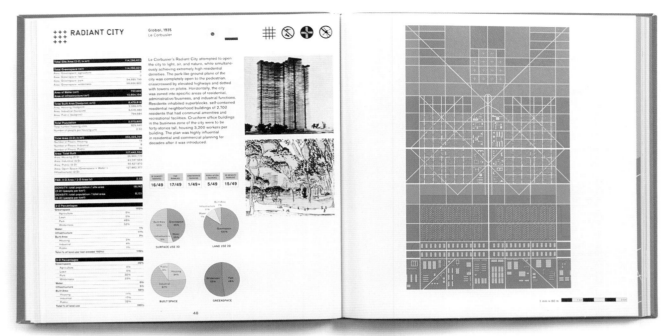

just aren't engaging cities in the same way. It has become so much less projective: either theorized as the site of real estate and public policy or increasingly turned over to a renewed technocratic faith in data. Of course, Modernism ushered in so many transformations for cities, not always for the best, but that there was a sense that cities could be planned and designed, inviting architects to engage with questions around housing, infrastructure, mobility, and public space.

DX Today everything has become the same everywhere. There is the idea that the Generic City is interesting, but maybe the Generic City just sucks.

AA As architects we need to reengage cities, to find new

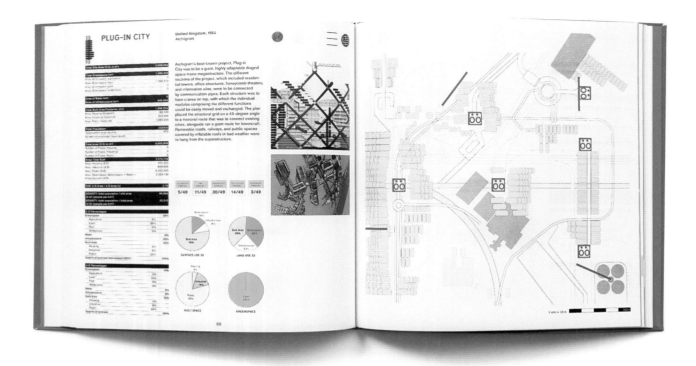

agency to project the city. I think that architects have shied away from that.

DX   In the face of sprawl, it has become harder to distinguish terms like "the city" and "urbanism." The traditional city had form—it had walls to define its edges, or a grid to give it order. Those qualities have been quite diluted.

AA   Right. You could make the argument that "the city" is what is designed and "urbanism" is what happens outside of that. It is made up of those conditions that are shaped by forces other than architects or planners. The boundary between those conditions is becoming so blurred that it is difficult to even establish the terminology, let alone tackle the problem.

DX   It is a relational issue of inside and out, and this is what we started addressing in *49 Cities*. We were looking just

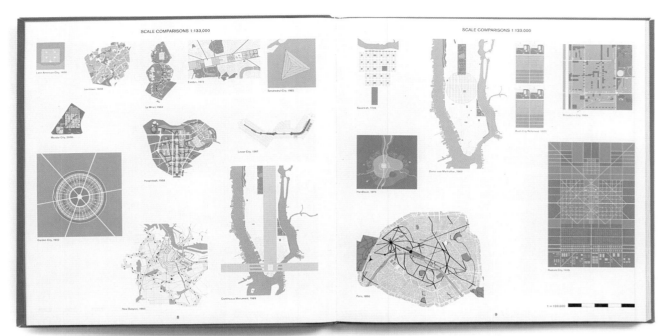

beyond the edges of the drawing to see how each city was imagined in its relationship to the world outside its walls.

__AA__   *49 Cities* took cities and made them more urban by connecting them to larger environmental concerns beyond their walls. We did this through representation, but also by looking at the cities' performance in terms of density, green space, etc. This also immediately informed our urban projects, like the Pingshan Master Plan, which became about infrastructure and connections to nature and systems, as well as about urban form.

In that sense, the loss of distinction between the city and urbanism can be productive: as if registering the difference between utopia and the realities of its construction. It's a blurring that works against "the city" as a formal autonomous entity, which is instead always already connected back to some sort of larger system. I think this same principle holds true for how we understand architecture.

173

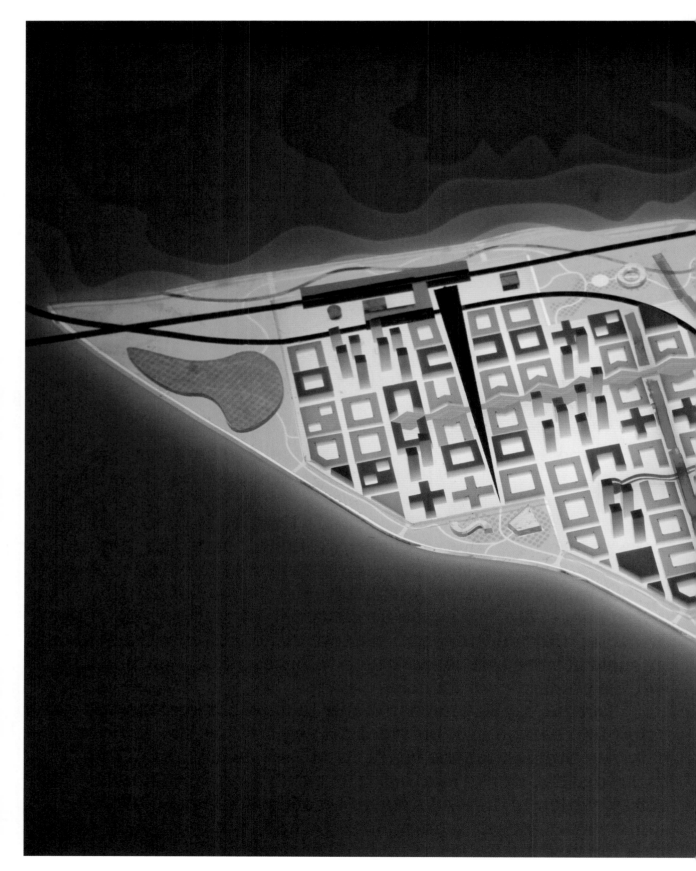

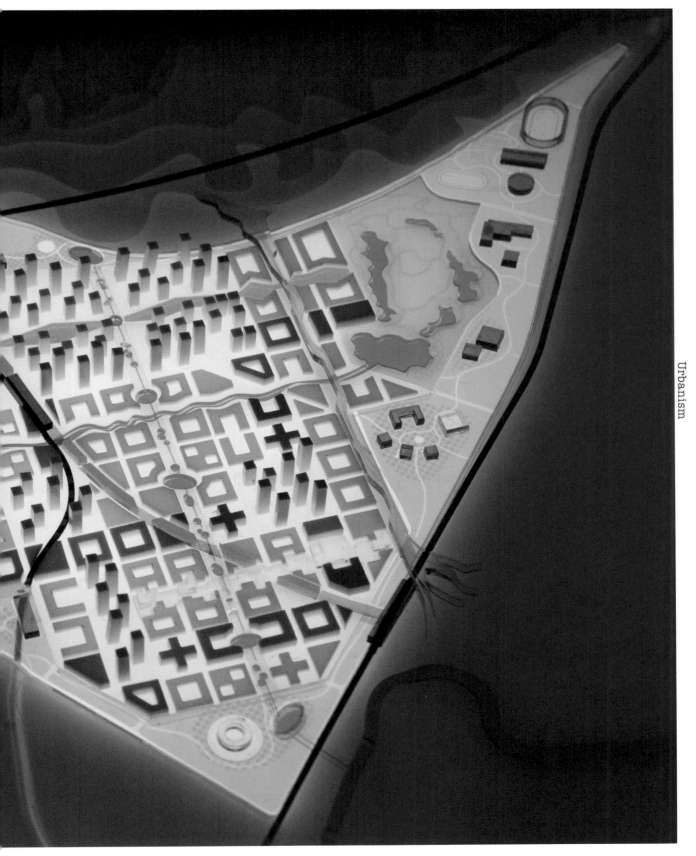

Urbanism

<u>DX</u>   In our urban projects, we have become increasingly interested in the relationship between our interventions and everything else around them. Green Belt City was a self-contained system, but by the time we designed Hua Qiang Bei Road, we had begun to develop projects integrated within larger infrastructural systems. With our proposal

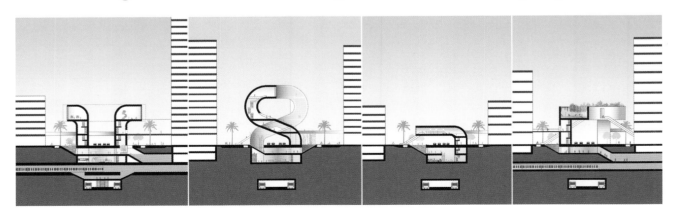

Urbanism

for the Beijing Horticultural Expo, designed together with SCAPE, Zhu Pei, and SLAB, we expanded our focus to include larger regional systems of water supply and other natural resources.

AA   It's true that almost all of our projects have integration at heart. We could have never done PF1 without what we learned from *49 Cities*. That research helped us clarify possible relationships between architecture and the environment, in terms of systems and infrastructure.

DX   Working on the campus plans in Weifang, in collaboration with the Horticultural Expo team, we first designed seven new campuses, then zoomed in to design one campus in detail— and are now working on the main library. At least for us, it is easier to think and work at the large scale and then translate it down to the small scale.

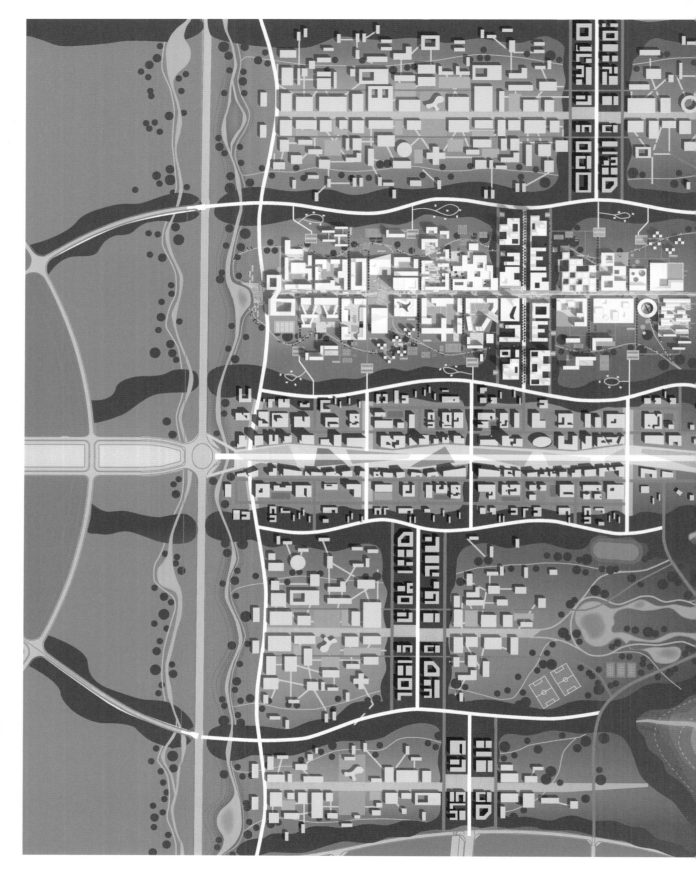

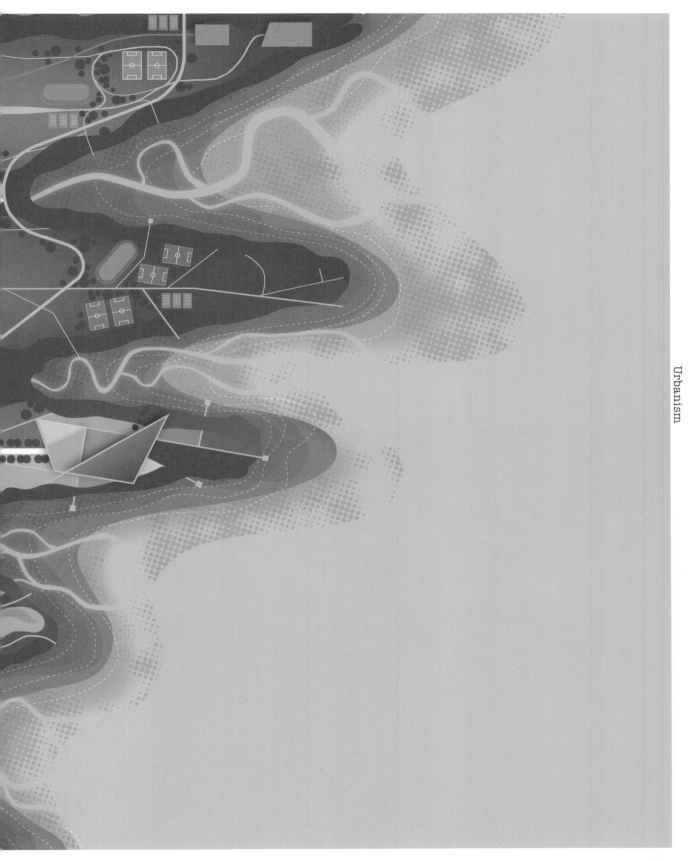

182

But working in the opposite way, like we did for the Silk Road competition where the building interprets Istanbul's historical layers spatially, can be a more tactical strategy as well.

AA   I think this conflation of city and urbanism is a two-way street. On one hand it is a way of connecting the city to those things—systems, infrastructures, nature—that have traditionally been thought of and designed as "outside" of how architecture has addressed the

city. On the other hand it is also a way of introducing *design* to those urban developments beyond the traditional image of the city and that previously fell outside of the jurisdiction of the architect. If we generalized urbanism as that set of conditions not designed, planned, or otherwise informed by the architect, then we should claim it anew as something that we can and should be addressing.

AA   In 2012 we won a competition for a new diplomatic conference center in Libreville, Gabon, which would house the biannual gathering of heads of state for the African Union.

DX   We were immediately struck by the way Gabon had engaged with Modernism post-independence: as an optimistic vision that paralleled the development of the country.

AA   We wanted to channel that sense of optimism for the architecture of the project, but without nostalgia.

DX   The competition asked for the building to "represent" the country and its embrace of an emerging green, service-oriented economy as it moved away from a dependence on oil revenue. So we enlisted landscape and ecology as a way to do this, with Gabon being 90 percent unoccupied rainforest.

AA   The building itself is a circle with the main auditorium in the center. The perimeter is organized around three courtyards, which hold three different types of landscapes: savannas, mountains, and jungles. The roof is tilted to become the building's main facade, as one approaches from the city below and reads the gardens and the water collection in the middle. The roof becomes the symbol for the country.

DX   It rains every day there. There is no wind, no earthquakes, no solar orientation. All it does is pour rain several times a day.

AA   The building collects rainwater on the roof in an accessible water feature, which becomes a waterfall in the rainforest garden before settling in a cistern. The water is then used throughout the building as a grey water system.

DX   The entire building is louvered which allowed us to punch big windows behind it. Between the stone louvers and the exterior wall is a walkway that circulates around the entire building. At the end of the day you can grab your fellow president, your colleagues, or your enemies and have a more informal meeting as you walk around the gardens.

Libreville, Gabon

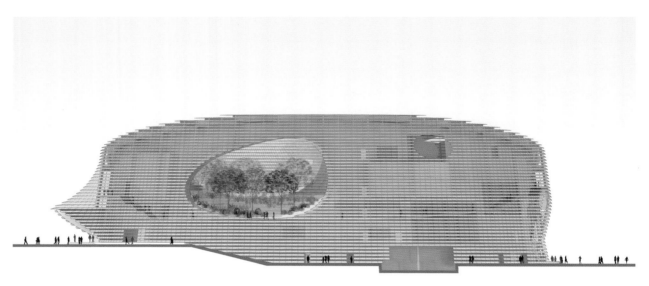

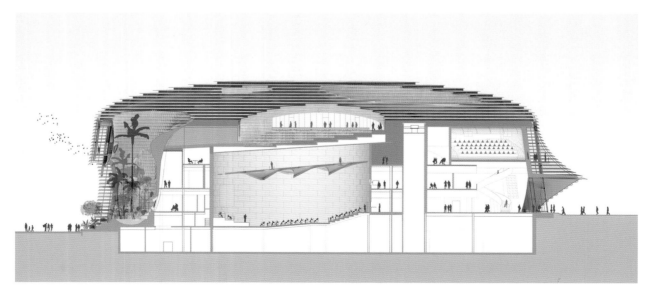

L'Assemblée Radieuse

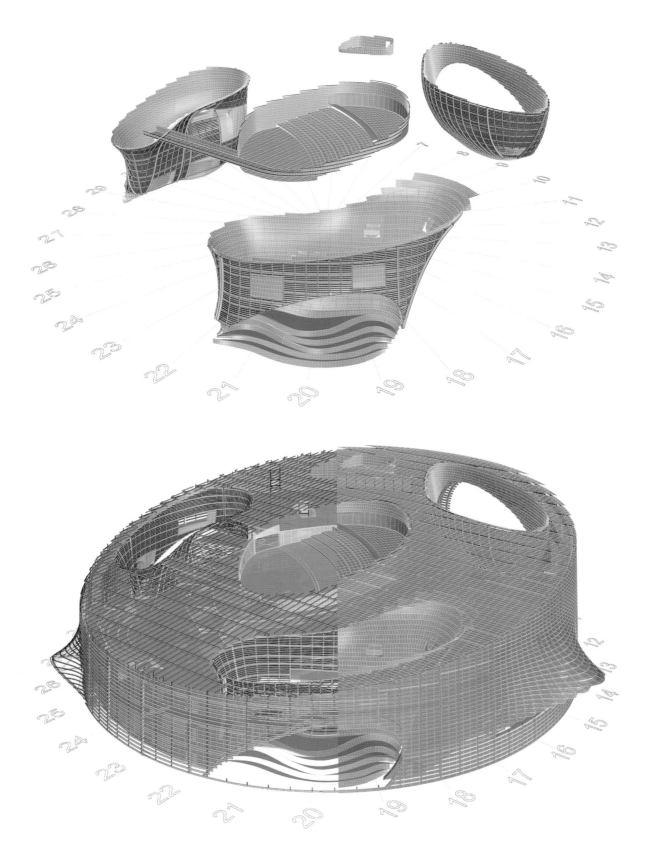

Libreville, Gabon

Walkway connecting conference
center to the banquet hall,
designed by Aranda\Lasch

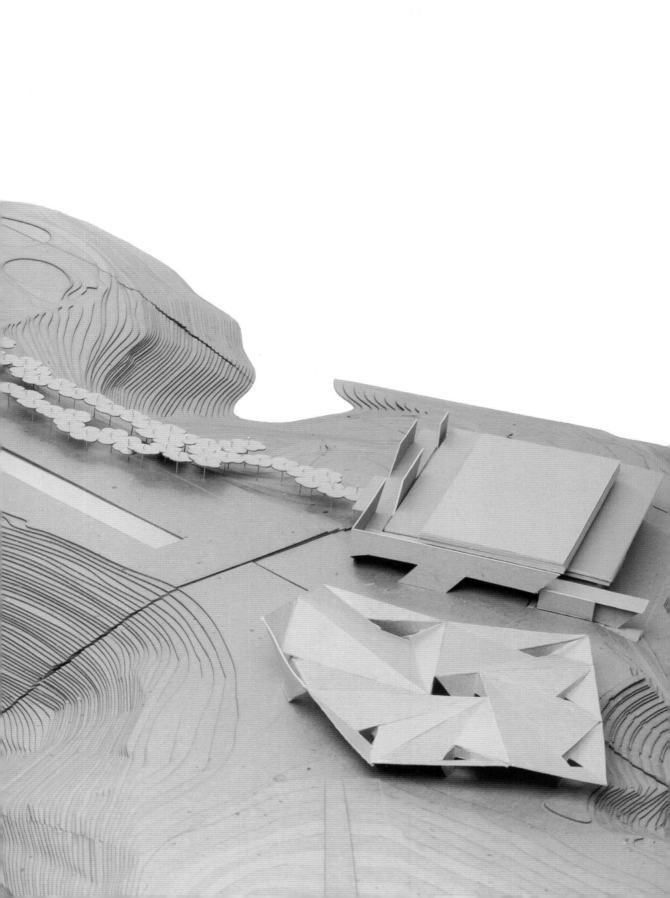

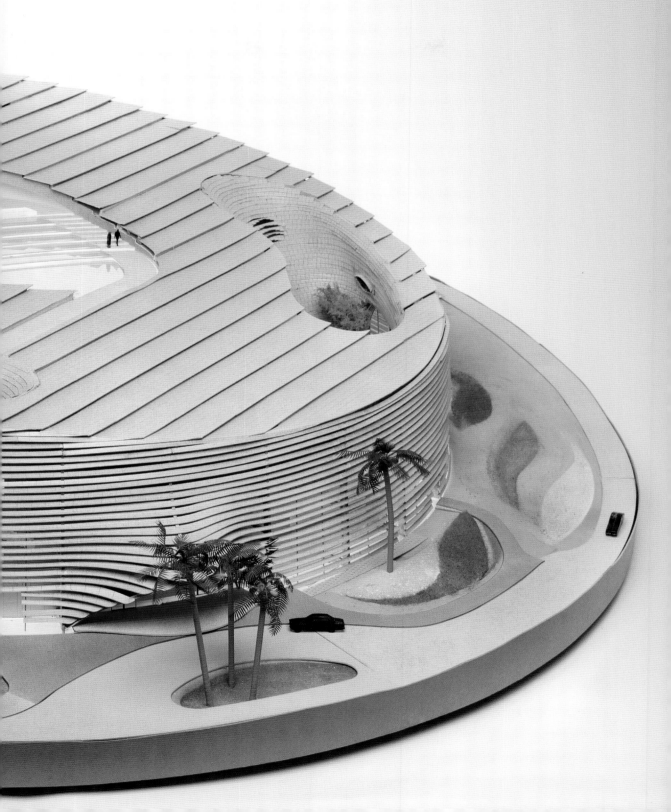

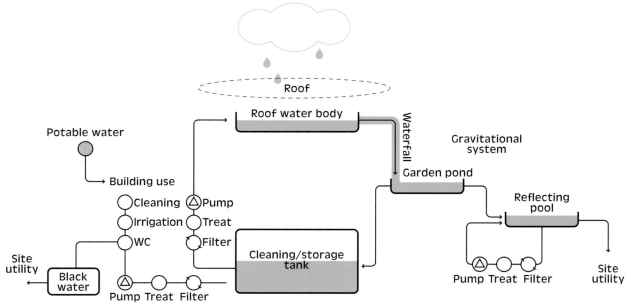

Libreville, Gabon

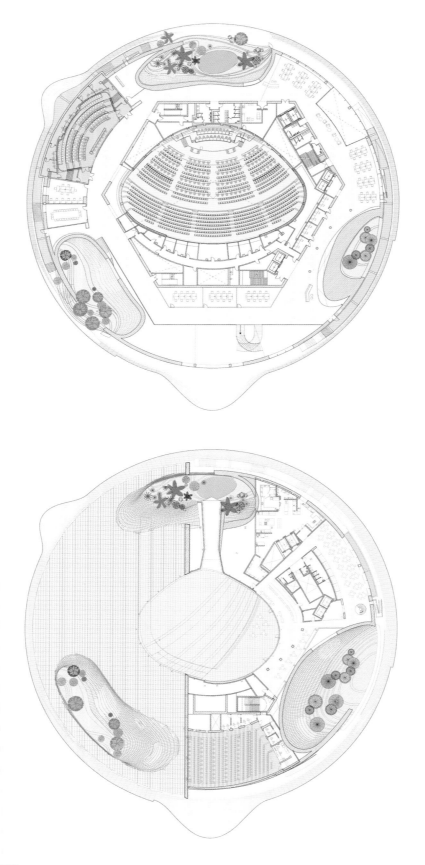

L'Assemblée Radieuse

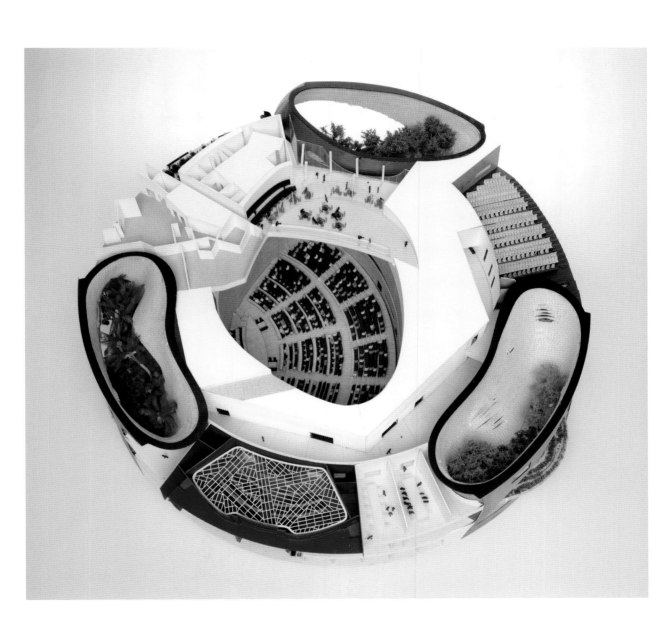

Libreville, Gabon

Libreville, Gabon

Libreville, Gabon

L'Assemblée Radieuse

Libreville, Gabon

Environments

<u>DX</u>   I think there are a few ways we look at nature in our work. The first is as a contrast between the built and the natural. Seeing plants in unexpected places, for instance, creates a new aesthetic experience, a sort of synaptic collapse.

<u>AA</u>   Contrast is incredibly important. Our interests in weaving together the built and the natural work against the idea of the landform building, for example, as a type. There is no contrast in a landform building. It conflates the built and the natural and kills any productive tension.

<u>DX</u>   Which is why we like objects.

<u>AA</u>   Yes. An object has resistance. Both "built" and "natural" are treated as objects that are juxtaposed. It is not about staging an opposition or allowing one to take over the other. It is about one framing the other and vice versa.

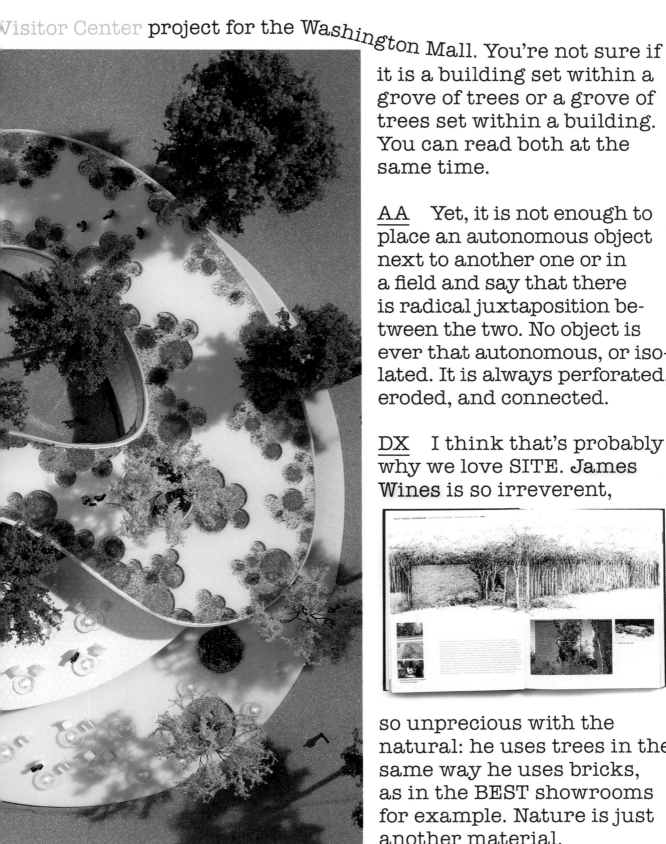

project for the Washington Mall. You're not sure if it is a building set within a grove of trees or a grove of trees set within a building. You can read both at the same time.

<u>AA</u>   Yet, it is not enough to place an autonomous object next to another one or in a field and say that there is radical juxtaposition between the two. No object is ever that autonomous, or isolated. It is always perforated, eroded, and connected.

<u>DX</u>   I think that's probably why we love SITE. James Wines is so irreverent,

so unprecious with the natural: he uses trees in the same way he uses bricks, as in the BEST showrooms for example. Nature is just another material.

AA   Yes. I think SITE's work certainly informs the way we are always trying to erode the object. I'm thinking of the gardens slicing through the UC Davis museum project, for example, inserting trees, texture, and outdoor spaces within a more abstract shell. It is a way of making the object real, of moving it away from the abstract and making it real.

DX   That's also why we are drawn to the idea of *productive* nature, the idea that nature can actually perform as part of architectural, urban, and ecological systems. That would be the other strain in our work.

AA   And when nature actually performs, it's interesting because it is not a pure form of nature. It's "second nature." That embrace of an unnatural or man-made nature is also important to us; it's really the contemporary condition.

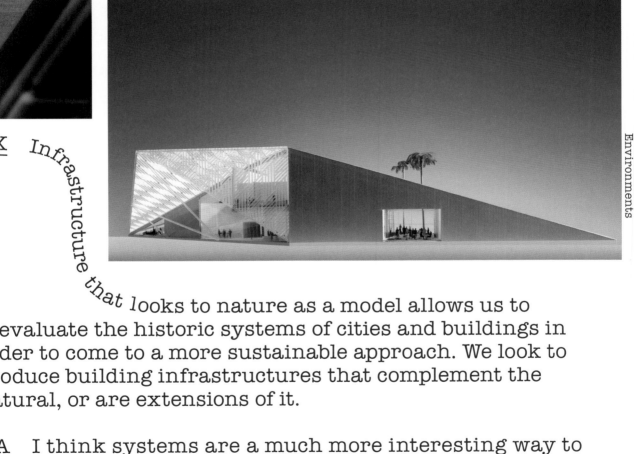

<u>DX</u> *Infrastructure that* looks to nature as a model allows us to reevaluate the historic systems of cities and buildings in order to come to a more sustainable approach. We look to produce building infrastructures that complement the natural, or are extensions of it.

<u>AA</u> I think systems are a much more interesting way to connect the built with the natural than something more formal, like biomorphism. Look at Paolo Soleri's projects, for instance. In *49 Cities*, despite all of Soleri's theories about Arcology and its naturalistic efficiencies, we discovered

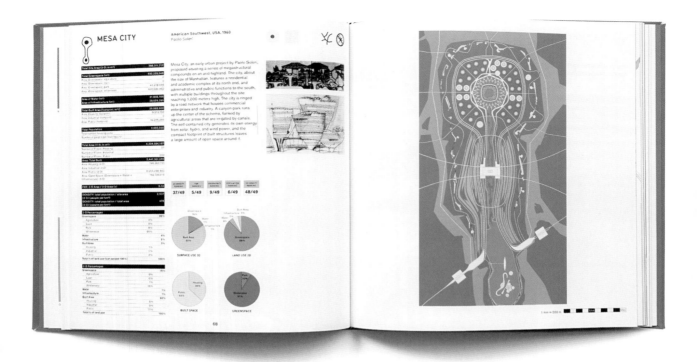

that Mesa City performs much worse than Radiant City in terms of density and footprint, despite looking more "natural" and organic. We would rather have it the other way around.

DX   Right. It's not as if we want to *represent* the "natural" or the "sustainable." The Swindler Cove Boathouse, for example, is all right angles, but it's also entirely porous and allows floodwaters and nature to flow around and through it. We are interested in systems and infrastructure as a way of shaping objects so that they can *perform* as part of a larger constructed natural system.

AA   Of course you can always design whatever you want and then slap solar panels on it, but it is much more interesting to address those same issues through form. Form should have more agency. A critic once commented that she wished there had been a window to the cistern of the Edible Schoolyard

NYC building at P.S. 216, in order to see what was inside. But why do you need a window if the *shape* of that part of the systems wall suggests what is happening inside? Why do you literally have to see it? Maybe we are more into phenomenological transparency as it relates to systems.

<u>DX</u> I think it is important to distinguish this sort of legibility from the biomorphic or landform buildings we were talking about earlier. Those types of buildings capitalize on representation, specifically on representing "nature." We aren't necessarily playing a game of representation. Legibility and representation are two different things.

<u>AA</u> Although I think the two can be mistaken for one another, and I think we play on that, sometimes. We have

done projects like the Shenda Tower or the Weifang Library, which are all about nature as a set of systems that work within the formal elements of the design—but we also do projects that represent the natural when it allows us to sidestep issues of cultural representation, such as in L'Assemblée Radieuse.

DX   It certainly is a much more comfortable way for us to engage culture. The concern with and enjoyment of the environment is inclusive. We really saw this with PF1. Gardening was such a shared passion among very diverse constituents. It was amazing to see how it could bring so many different types of people together.

AA   In a way, if you can't escape representation, then the environment is the best thing that you can represent because it has more potential for a shared ground and conversation.

2013–

Stuff the Envelope

2018

(post-oil-price crash)

We start 2013 with a forty-five-person office spread over two floors of our building on Ludlow Street. I travel to Gabon every six weeks or so. The project is managed by Bechtel, which has 400 people in Libreville staffing the Agence Nationale des Grands Travaux ("Big Projects Agency") for the Gabonese government. It is the fastest fast-track project we have ever worked on. We enlist an enormous team of consultants, engineers, and designers. Together with our partner, the Chicago A/E firm Epstein, we decide to complete the Construction Documents ourselves in New York. In 2014 we visit the site, where 900 people are already working. In a warehouse somewhere in Turkey there are 8,000 tons of steel waiting to be shipped. Then something happens. Maybe we should have listened when Arup refused to proceed after Design Development. They were right. We were wrong. As oil prices crash, the Gabonese economy follows. The President fights for reelection and the project goes on hold. Our bills go unpaid, our phone calls unanswered.

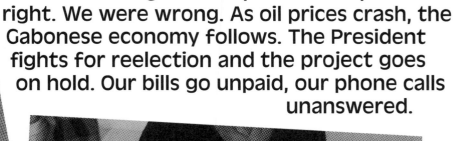

We start the inevitable layoffs and belt-tightening. In New York, however, things are moving. Our offices for Wieden+Kennedy are completed as perhaps the pinnacle of our engagement with

interiors. Our first developer project, the Stealth Building, opens up new ways of thinking about preservation. We complete the second Edible Schoolyard NYC, in East Harlem. Having left Princeton in 2011, Amale becomes a tenure-track professor at Columbia GSAPP. That track takes a sudden swerve and she becomes the dean in 2014. I teach at Yale, Cornell,

and Penn, and we rethink how the office and our lives can be organized. We begin turning down project after project in order to be able to concentrate together in the small windows of time at the office. We were wrong about that as well. The office shrinks even further. Amale is unhappy with most of the decisions made in her absence. There is at least a year of bad design and bad moods. In 2016, with Amale entering her third year as dean, things begin to stabilize at the school, the skies clear, and the energy in the office improves. For our garage project in Miami, we rediscover some of the ideas developed in our earliest interior projects to reconceptualize the building envelope, thickening it while adopting a new exuberance. That provides the design spark for the projects that follow. During a six-month period in 2016 we finish seven competitions and speculative projects. The guest-house in Arizona, the Museum of Sex expansion, the Adirondacks Distillery, and a series of competitions

including the Women's Building in Chelsea, the Dreamquarters in Toronto, the new Four Seasons, and our entry for a new museum in Beirut usher in a renewed focus on architecture. We lose all of the competitions (and a couple of projects) but it's worth it. We enter 2017 with three employees and by the end of the year are back up to twenty. We are getting used to this.

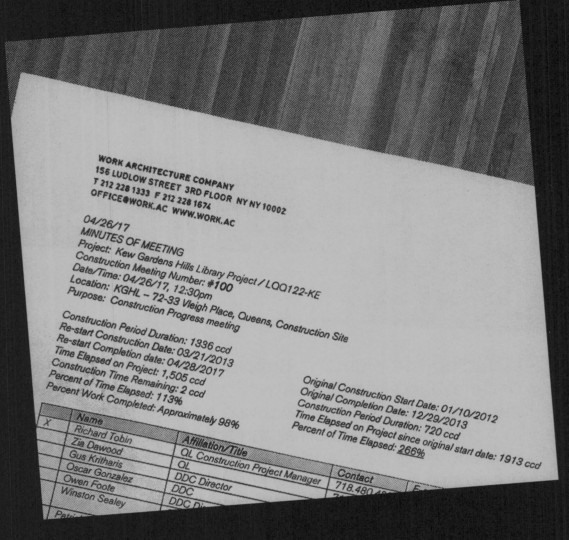

WORK ARCHITECTURE COMPANY
156 LUDLOW STREET 3RD FLOOR NY NY 10002
T 212 228 1333 F 212 228 1674
OFFICE@WORK.AC WWW.WORK.AC

04/26/17
MINUTES OF MEETING
Project: Kew Gardens Hills Library Project / LQQ122-KE
Construction Meeting Number: #100
Date/Time: 04/26/17, 12:30pm
Location: KGHL ~ 72-33 Vleigh Place, Queens, Construction Site
Purpose: Construction Progress meeting

Construction Period Duration: 1336 ccd
Re-start Construction Date: 03/21/2013
Re-start Completion date: 04/28/2017
Time Elapsed on Project: 1,505 ccd
Construction Time Remaining: 2 ccd
Percent of Time Elapsed: 113%
Percent Work Completed: Approximately 98%

Original Construction Start Date: 01/10/2012
Original Completion Date: 12/29/2013
Construction Period Duration: 720 ccd
Time Elapsed on Project since original start date: 1913 ccd
Percent of Time Elapsed: 266%

X	Name	Affiliation/Title	Contact	
	Richard Tobin			
	Zia Dawood	QL Construction Project Manager		
	Gus Kritharis	QL	718.480	
	Oscar Gonzalez	DDC Director		
	Owen Foote	DDC		
	Winston Sealey	DDC Di		
	Patri			

Every other week at the site meeting for our
Kew Gardens Hills Library, we review the minutes
from the previous meeting.

At the top is the number of days of construction.
As of writing, it is 1,913 days . . . and counting.

—Dan Wood

AA   Workplace design is like landscape architecture for interiors. There is, of course, the cubicle, but then there are those radical Chiat/Day experiments where no one had a desk and everything was mobile. Today the tech world has really fallen into a model of work-as-play.

DX   But work is work. And for a creative advertising agency like Wieden+Kennedy, work already can and should be fun without needing to be themed as a playground, like they have done at Google.

AA   Part of our initial investigation for Wieden+Kennedy was to study how they worked in and occupied their space. The office was initially very call center–like: an open work environment that wasted space in terms of the simplest things, like the distances between desks and columns. Density became really important. How could we shrink the individual spaces enough to maximize the collective spaces? The typology and scale of these different workspaces became critical.

DX   Instead of focusing on theme we focused on work: how you meet, where and for how long as a way to create a variety of meeting rooms, from small, to big, to really big, which involved carving the actual building in various ways.

AA   There's the cut for the coin stair that connects all three floors and there's also the double-height outdoor courtyard which creates interesting and unexpected connections between floors and between inside and outside.

DX   We have done quite a number of offices, but this is our most successful for sure.

AA   It's hard to imagine outdoing that collaboration.

Hudson Square, New York

Hudson Square, New York

Wieden+Kennedy

Hudson Square, New York

Wieden+Kennedy

Hudson Square, New York

Work Culture

DX Work is something we have always thought about, and it inspired our name. We have been interested in the way other people work, whether they are caterers, jewelry makers, or fashion designers.

AA Our expectations about work environments have changed so much from the Modernist sea of generic cubicles. The cubicle addressed the question of productivity, but today there is a new set of questions that revolves around creativity and wellbeing. Take Gaetano Pesce's radical rethinking of the work environment as a domestic setting or Apple's beginnings in a garage and you wonder what makes a creative work environment. It is just a loft? Is it a warehouse? There is still

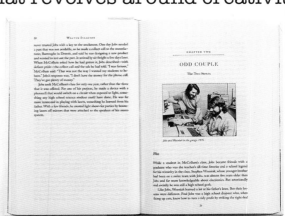

241

this sense that designed work spaces should be as generic and flexible as possible, that one size fits all. To find that balance between the generic and the specific, between the flexible and the fixed, has been quite interesting for us.

<u>DX</u> Flexibility is one of the big myths of office planning and working. Nobody really wants flexibility because it is so banal. The proposition is that every space can serve every purpose, but none of those spaces do any one thing very well.

<u>AA</u> Flexibility is also exhausting for people trying to work in that space. It becomes another decision that needs to be made. Consider the very creative people who eat the same thing everyday to reduce the number of decisions they need to make and be free to think about other things.

<u>DX</u> We're not opposed to flexibility, it just means something very different to us.

<u>AA</u> It is not an endless sprawl of possibilities. As at Wieden+ Kennedy, it is a density of possibilities: fixed rooms instead of flexible cubicles.

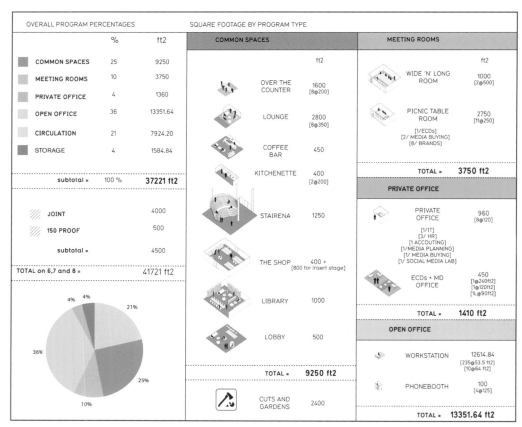

OVERALL PROGRAM PERCENTAGES		
	%	ft2
COMMON SPACES	25	9250
MEETING ROOMS	10	3750
PRIVATE OFFICE	4	1360
OPEN OFFICE	36	13351.64
CIRCULATION	21	7924.20
STORAGE	4	1584.84
subtotal =	100 %	37221 ft2
JOINT		4000
150 PROOF		500
subtotal =		4500
TOTAL on 6,7 and 8 =		41721 ft2

SQUARE FOOTAGE BY PROGRAM TYPE

COMMON SPACES

		ft2
	OVER THE COUNTER	1600 [8@200]
	LOUNGE	2800 [8@350]
	COFFEE BAR	450
	KITCHENETTE	400 [2@200]
	STAIRENA	1250
	THE SHOP	400 + [800 for insert stage]
	LIBRARY	1000
	LOBBY	500
	TOTAL =	9250 ft2
	CUTS AND GARDENS	2400

MEETING ROOMS

		ft2
	WIDE 'N' LONG ROOM	1000 [2@500]
	PICNIC TABLE ROOM	2750 [11@250]
		[1/ECDs] [2/ MEDIA BUYING] [8/ BRANDS]
	TOTAL =	3750 ft2

PRIVATE OFFICE

	PRIVATE OFFICE	960 [8@120]
		[1/IT] [3/ HR] [1 ACCOUTING] [1/MEDIA PLANNING] [1/ MEDIA BUYING] [1/ SOCIAL MEDIA LAB]
	ECDs + MD OFFICE	450 [1@240ft2] [1@120ft2] [1L@90ft2]
	TOTAL =	1410 ft2

OPEN OFFICE

	WORKSTATION	12614.84 [235@53.5 ft2] [10@64 ft2]
	PHONEBOOTH	100 [4@125]
	TOTAL =	13351.64 ft2

DX We don't assume that every space can be everything. The workspaces we design are pretty specific, but we like to design enough variety in that specificity so that no matter what space you need, there is something close to that available. That is why its about density and difference rather than flexibility.

AA We would like to reclaim architecture in the work place. At a certain point, in the name of flexibility, workplace architecture

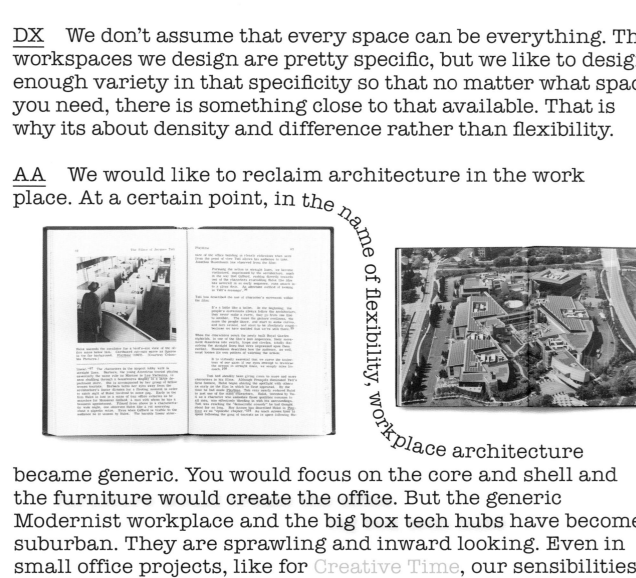

became generic. You would focus on the core and shell and the furniture would create the office. But the generic Modernist workplace and the big box tech hubs have become suburban. They are sprawling and inward looking. Even in small office projects, like for Creative Time, our sensibilities are more urban, which suggests an attention to scale.

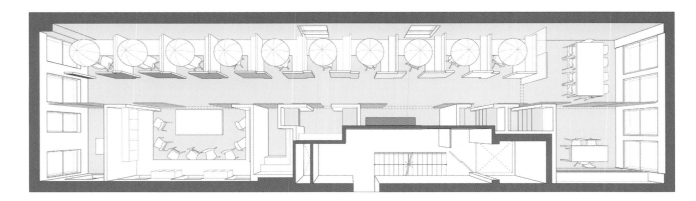

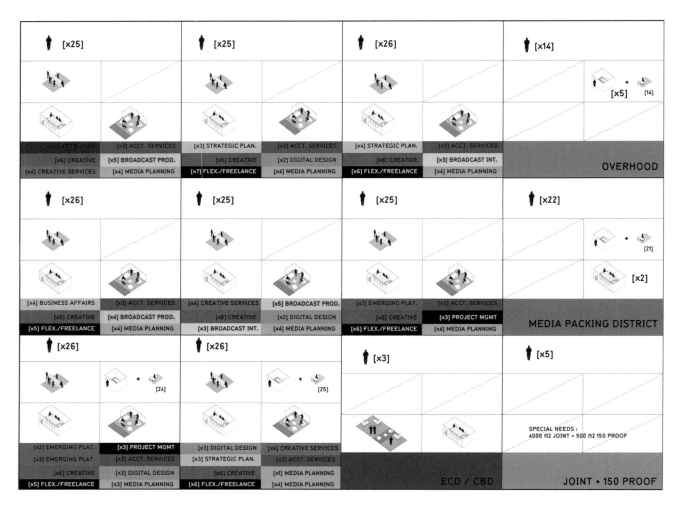

[x25]	[x25]	[x26]	[x14]
[x3] ART BUYING · [x3] ACCT. SERVICES	[x3] STRATEGIC PLAN. · [x3] ACCT. SERVICES	[x4] STRATEGIC PLAN. · [x3] ACCT. SERVICES	[x5] + [14]
[x6] CREATIVE · [x5] BROADCAST PROD.	[x6] CREATIVE · [x2] DIGITAL DESIGN	[x6] CREATIVE · [x3] BROADCAST INT.	
[x4] CREATIVE SERVICES · [x4] MEDIA PLANNING	[x7] FLEX./FREELANCE · [x4] MEDIA PLANNING	[x6] FLEX./FREELANCE · [x4] MEDIA PLANNING	**OVERHOOD**
[x26]	**[x25]**	**[x25]**	**[x22]**
[x4] BUSINESS AFFAIRS · [x3] ACCT. SERVICES	[x4] CREATIVE SERVICES · [x5] BROADCAST PROD.	[x3] EMERGING PLAT. · [x3] ACCT. SERVICES	[21] + [x2]
[x6] CREATIVE · [x4] BROADCAST PROD.	[x6] CREATIVE · [x2] DIGITAL DESIGN	[x6] CREATIVE · [x3] PROJECT MGMT	
[x5] FLEX./FREELANCE · [x4] MEDIA PLANNING	[x3] BROADCAST INT. · [x4] MEDIA PLANNING	[x6] FLEX./FREELANCE · [x4] MEDIA PLANNING	**MEDIA PACKING DISTRICT**
[x26]	**[x26]**	**[x3]**	**[x5]**
[24] · [x2] EMERGING PLAT. · [x3] PROJECT MGMT	[25] · [x3] DIGITAL DESIGN · [x4] CREATIVE SERVICES		SPECIAL NEEDS : 4000 ft2 JOINT + 500 ft2 150 PROOF
[x3] EMERGING PLAT. · [x3] ACCT. SERVICES	[x3] STRATEGIC PLAN. · [x3] ACCT. SERVICES		
[x6] CREATIVE · [x3] DIGITAL DESIGN	[x6] CREATIVE · [x1] MEDIA PLANNING		
[x5] FLEX./FREELANCE · [x3] MEDIA PLANNING	[x6] FLEX./FREELANCE · [x4] MEDIA PLANNING	**ECD / CBD**	**JOINT + 150 PROOF**

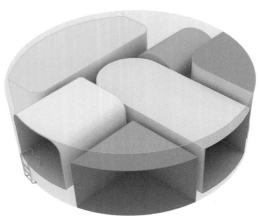

For Wieden+Kennedy, we looked to produce variation by probing the way people work now. Not all meetings are the same, for instance. For KBS+,

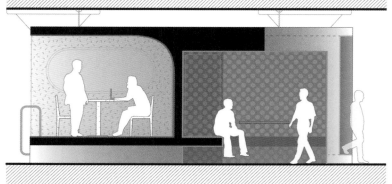

we created spaces for different scales of meetings in terms of time and space. On an

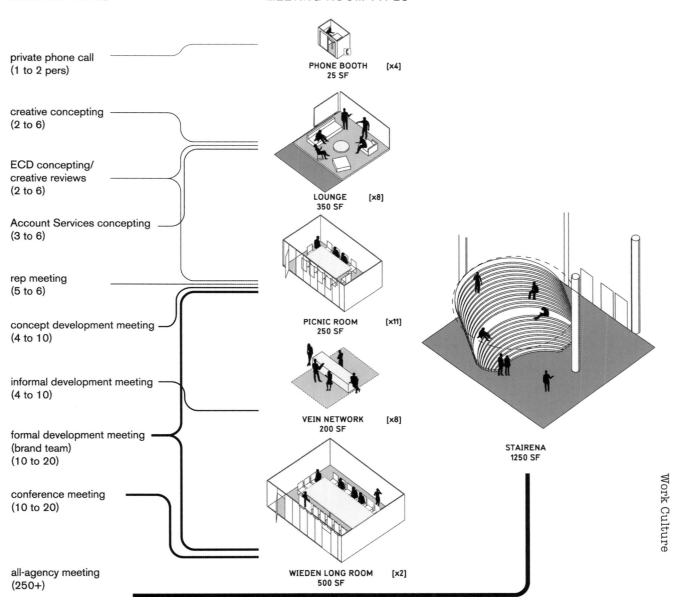

private phone call
(1 to 2 pers)

creative concepting
(2 to 6)

ECD concepting/
creative reviews
(2 to 6)

Account Services concepting
(3 to 6)

rep meeting
(5 to 6)

concept development meeting
(4 to 10)

informal development meeting
(4 to 10)

formal development meeting
(brand team)
(10 to 20)

conference meeting
(10 to 20)

all-agency meeting
(250+)

PHONE BOOTH   [x4]
25 SF

LOUNGE   [x8]
350 SF

PICNIC ROOM   [x11]
250 SF

VEIN NETWORK   [x8]
200 SF

STAIRENA
1250 SF

WIEDEN LONG ROOM   [x2]
500 SF

Work Culture

architectural level that variation is really interesting. You need a big and a small rather than two medium-sized things. Instead of producing a sprawl of scalar sameness, we are trying to produce contained difference.

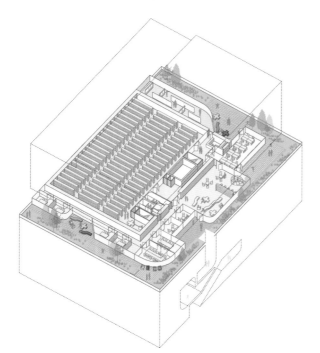

DX   You can see in the Guggenheim Collection Center project how our interest in verticality also plays into this. Fifty thousand feet spread out

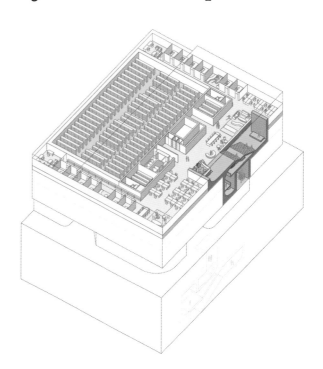

over one floor means that you have this sprawling horizontal environment to deal with. You have no idea what is going on at the other end of your floor. Its all open, but it's also very isolating, sort of like the suburbs. Once you introduce a vertical element you produce a whole new set of ways for people to interact with one another. For one, it's a shorter distance to move up rather than across, but also elements like stairs become places where you can meet, where you

are able to see what other people are doing, or at least have a sense. That's impossible in a horizontal environment, thus the importance of creating section, such as in our competition for the Women's Building.

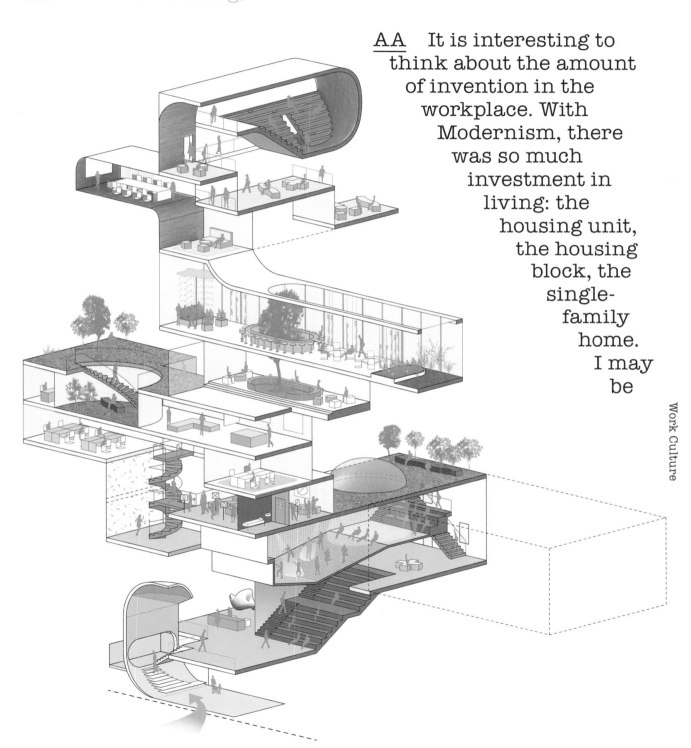

<u>AA</u> It is interesting to think about the amount of invention in the workplace. With Modernism, there was so much investment in living: the housing unit, the housing block, the single-family home. I may be

wrong, but the kind of post-industrial landscape of the work environment has not been as theorized. There has been invention, but not much critical thinking. And yet, in a city like New York, the residential typology is copying the commercial one. Luxury residential towers are all glass, borrowing from office buildings; WeWork launched WeLive. As work has infiltrated life, life is learning from work. The work models are starting to change life models.

DX   With our project for the Dreamquarters in Toronto, we saw how people are much more willing to experiment with their workplace than they are with their house or apartment. That is what was so great with our commercial clients in the early days. They had no money, no time, the spaces weren't great, but they were open to any idea that you had. It was very fun.

AA   We should write a book about work culture. While "work" has been heavily historicized as fundamental to the history of Modernism, contemporary work cultures are rarely placed in that kind of context.

Stealth Building

Tribeca, New York
2011–16

DX   What's great about working in New York is that there are processes such as those of the Department of Buildings and the Landmarks Preservation Commission that allow for the presentation of an argument. Preservation, for example, does not always mean a complete embrace of the past.

AA   The Stealth Building on Reade Street was a great opportunity for us to engage preservation in a creative way. It's a residential development that's partly a renovation of an existing building and partly an addition of a two-and-a-half-story penthouse. We are finding that transforming existing structures is not only one of the most sustainable ways to build—it also provides great opportunities for architectural invention.

DX   The crenellated roof form of the penthouse addition was entirely the result of being conscious of Landmarks requirements, of wanting to intervene in both visible and invisible ways. It's an exuberant form that was designed tracing the sightlines—as if a "shadow" cast by the building and its neighbor's pediments and bulkheads. From the street it is actually invisible!

AA   This created a topography for the penthouse roof which we wanted to carry through in other ways to the simplex apartments below.

DX   For each apartment, we reworked the kitchen/bathrooms core to create an object with a stepped, terraced roof that hosts a sleeping loft, an herb garden, and a mini-greenhouse connected to the master shower, where ferns grow as a result of the shower's steam.

AA   Where we couldn't insert plants, we created patterns, such as for the bathroom walls.

DX   It's again about a density of microenvironments and experiences, in an almost Japanese way.

AA   On the exterior, we found the existing cast-iron facade to be incredibly beautiful. It's blackness and proportions made it stand out like an art piece on the street. We wanted to preserve this quality but also reinterpret it by collaborating with the artist Michael Hansmeyer to produce an original Corinthian capital. All of the original capitals had been lost. It was the first time Landmarks ever allowed a contemporary design as part of a facade restoration.

DX   It's amazing because from the street at first glance you wouldn't really know that we did anything.

AA   That's kind of the point.

Tribeca, New York

Stealth Building

Tribeca, New York

Tribeca, New York

Stealth Building

Stealth Building

Tribeca, New York

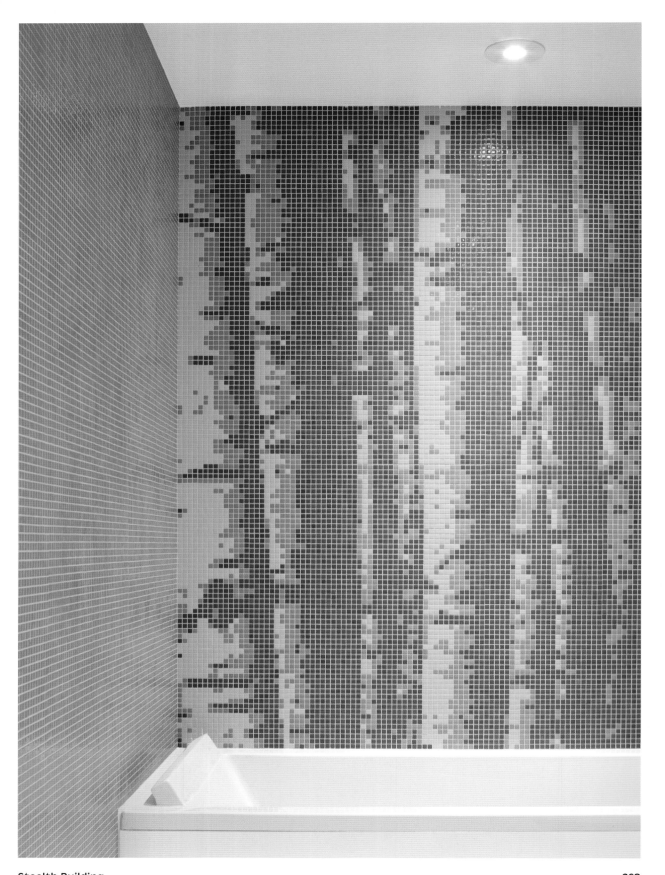

Stealth Building

Tribeca, New York

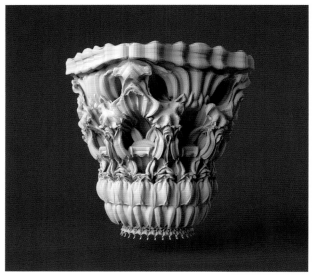

Stealth Building

In collaboration with Michael Hansmeyer

Tribeca, New York

Preservation

DX For our Stealth building we made an argument to Landmarks that one can never accurately know an "original" or "authentic" condition and therefore what is new should be different and not an attempt to replicate an unknowable past. That encapsulates our thinking about preservation in general.

AA Cadavre Exquis Lebanese, our theoretical proposal for downtown Beirut, is an interesting lens through which to look at some of our other preservation projects. It was set in contrast to the actual reconstruction master plan, which assigned values to buildings according to what they were supposed to represent. It became a fiction of a city coming together beyond its religious differences, while actually constructing those differences through preservation. For our proposal, the question of whether a building was Ottoman or French, a mosque, a church, or a temple was irrelevant. Rather, we focused on overarching infrastructures and the spaces between buildings as a way to stitch the city's fabric back together: new zones, historic sites, or even archaeological digs.

DX   We also polemically proposed to create new buildings based on "iconic programs." It was a bit like the "I am a monument" sketch in *Learning from Las Vegas* in that we were taking the everyday and monumentalizing it. We created monuments to Lebanese cuisine, smoking hookahs, nonsectarian public education. . . .

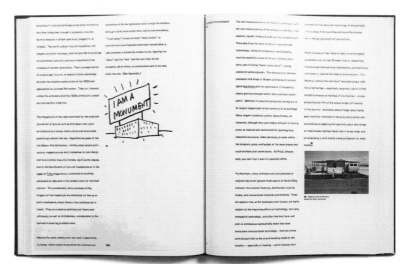

AA   The project became an assortment of things that collapsed hierarchical cultural values, and we became increasingly skeptical of certain notions of authenticity or cultural representation that are often implied in questions of preservation and cultural heritage. We were more interested in introducing new lines of inquiry that could reveal other narratives and construct alternate histories.

I have always been fascinated with this idea of the ruin for this reason. Its layered archaeologies and multiple narratives. You don't want to disrupt that with any single reading. You have to be surgical, a bit stealthy.

DX   This is especially significant for New Holland Island in Saint Petersburg. It had been abandoned for decades as a sort of void in the city, with another void at its center, the testing pool. We were intrigued by this notion of nesting and subtraction. Our project positioned itself against Foster's 2004 scheme for the island, which was all about addition: new buildings around the perimeter and a big concert hall in the middle, to fill the void of

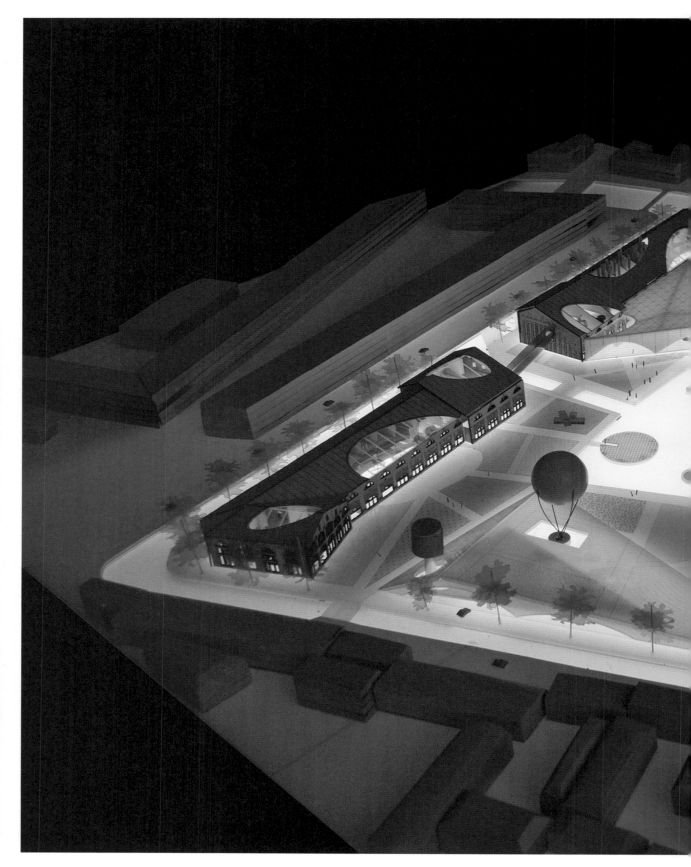

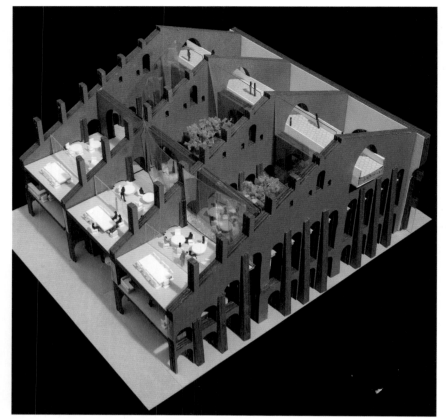

AA   Our question was: What is the least we could do with the most impact?

DX   Which led to the idea of carving the mass of the warehouses, just enough to introduce other programs and allow the park to move inside in wintertime.

AA   The preservationists were focused on preserving the exteriors when, in fact, it was the interiors that had contributed most to the island's history. Our intervention channeled a Matta-Clark strategy of subtraction, where the inside is opened up and allowed to reconnect with the city outside.

DX   Even the new museum building is both a continuation of the landscape on one side, and the city fabric and a new civic facade on the other.

<u>AA</u>　For Diane von Furstenberg Studio Headquarters, on the other hand, our addition is completely visible. This was tied to a specific notion of interiors and exteriors in New York.

For landmarked buildings, the insides are allowed to change

pression of this difference, something that made the schism between interior and exterior that Koolhaas rendered paradigmatic of New York in his reading of the Downtown Athletic Club more legible.

but the facades have to remain. We saw the addition as an ex

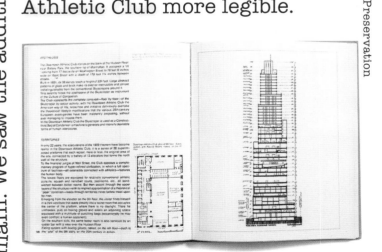

This is even more clear in our addition to the Blaffer Art Museum, where the new circulation and organization actually frames and emphasizes the entrance in what had been a blank brick wall.

<u>DX</u> For this reason, I take issue with Diller Scofidio + Renfro's argument for not keeping the facade of the Folk Art Museum as part of their new extension for MoMA. They said it would be "facade-ism" to preserve it, because the inside was going to change. But there was never a clear relationship

between the inside and the outside of that building in the

first place—there rarely is in urban buildings—so why not keep it as an important historic artifact?

<u>AA</u> It's an interesting point because ultimately when you deal with preservation you are making an argument for an approach for which you have to construct a compelling narrative. What time period are you taking something back to and why? Narrative is the medium of preservationists. Presenting to Landmarks is making a case for an interesting narrative that is multilayered and expands one's understanding of an object or a site, rather than limits it. New York is a

very rich city to be dealing with preservation because it is always reinventing itself from the inside.

AA   This project started as a response to the glass towers that are taking over cities around the world, including Beirut. Part of the fallout of this is the loss of the balcony, which performs climatically, but is also a beautiful transitional device not only between inside and outside, but also between private space and public space.

DX   In Lebanon, a new law also allows people to enclose their balconies, which only exacerbates the problem. We wanted to find a way to revive the balcony, not so literally as an architectural element but as a charged urban space of social exchange.

Maurizio Bianchi Mattioli There is something about the grain of the city as well. The glass towers are eradicating a certain scale from the city. Everything is being scaled up. With this project we were not only trying to revive the balcony, but also a smaller, more organic scale that is quickly disappearing from Beirut.

AA   We wanted to compress our building as much as possible, not only to mitigate the scale of the building, but also to create a park for a city that is very much lacking in green-space.

DX   We discovered that the back-of-house spaces would only support 80 percent of the galleries they were planning for. Rather than enlarging the back-of-house spaces, we took out 20 percent of the gallery program and redistributed it within a thickened facade.

AA   These spaces become a vertical continuation of the park within the facade, and create a new kind of publicly accessible part of the city.

MB   More than just wrapping the museum's interior spaces, the envelope itself becomes a series of rooms.

DX   Inside, the galleries are very flexible and generic, in a way. They are shifted in section to differentiate between the museum's permanent and temporary collections so one can move up vertically and visit only the permanent collection or the temporary collection— or cross back and forth between the two.

AA   In plan you can read the erosion of the galleries by the outdoor rooms. The binary of reading the holes versus the solids disappears. It's like PF1 on ecstasy.

DX   PF1 *was* on ecstasy.

AA   Those were the days. . . .

Our collaboration with Maurizio Bianchi Mattioli began with the L'Assemblée Radieuse project in 2012. Since then, he has brought his design and leadership skills to bear on competitions such as the Beijing Horticultural Expo and the Beirut Museum of Art, master plans including the Weifang Campus Master Plan and Main Library and our current work on the Marea project in Batroun, Lebanon.

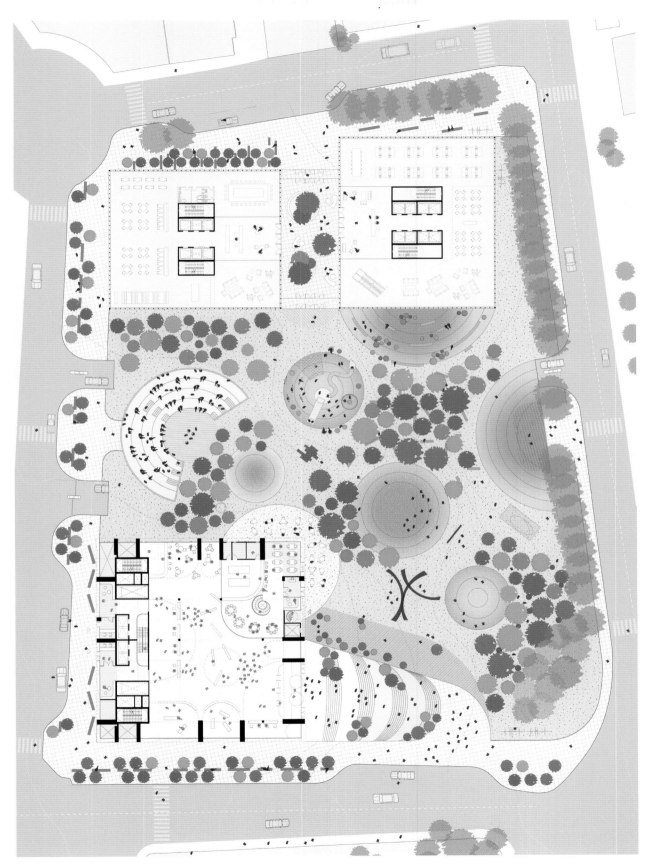

Beirut, Lebanon

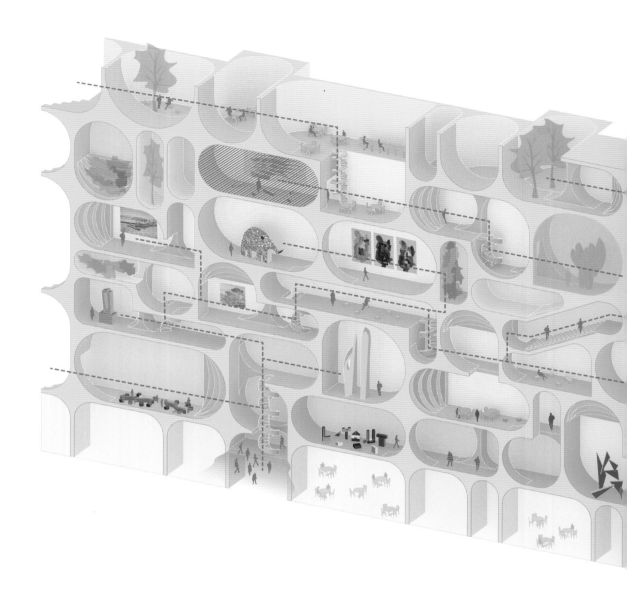

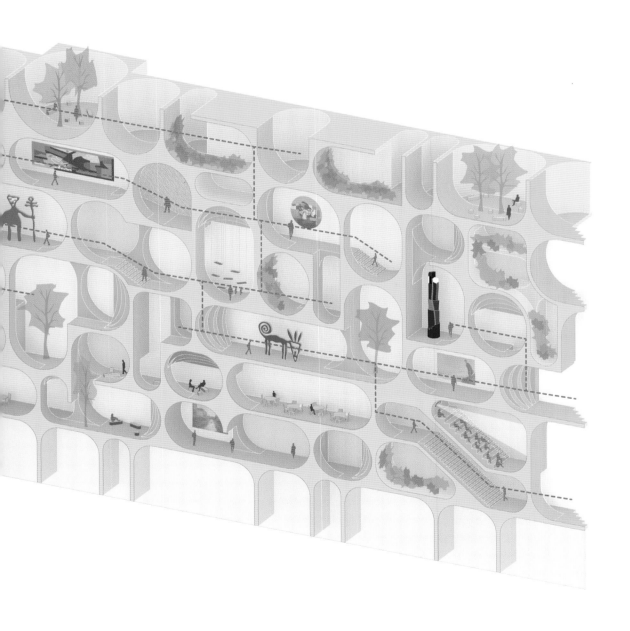

Beirut, Lebanon

Beirut Museum of Art

Beirut, Lebanon

Facade detail section

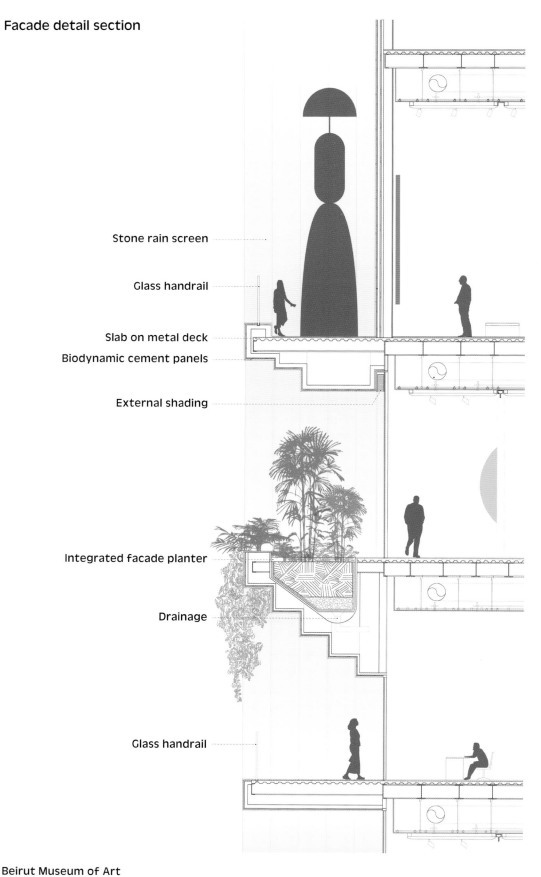

Stone rain screen

Glass handrail

Slab on metal deck

Biodynamic cement panels

External shading

Integrated facade planter

Drainage

Glass handrail

Level 1
Entrance and mezzanine

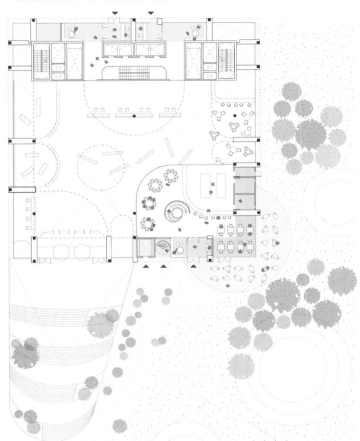

Level 2
Community art space

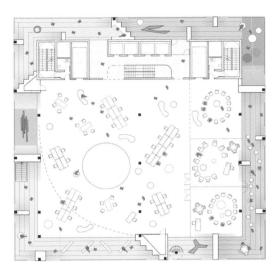

Level 6
Galleries

Level 7
Administration

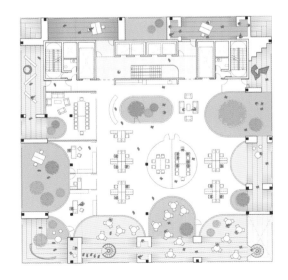

Beirut, Lebanon

Beirut Museum of Art

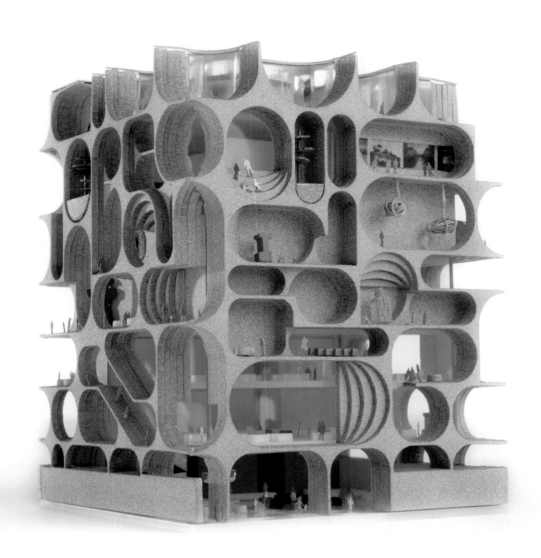

Beirut, Lebanon

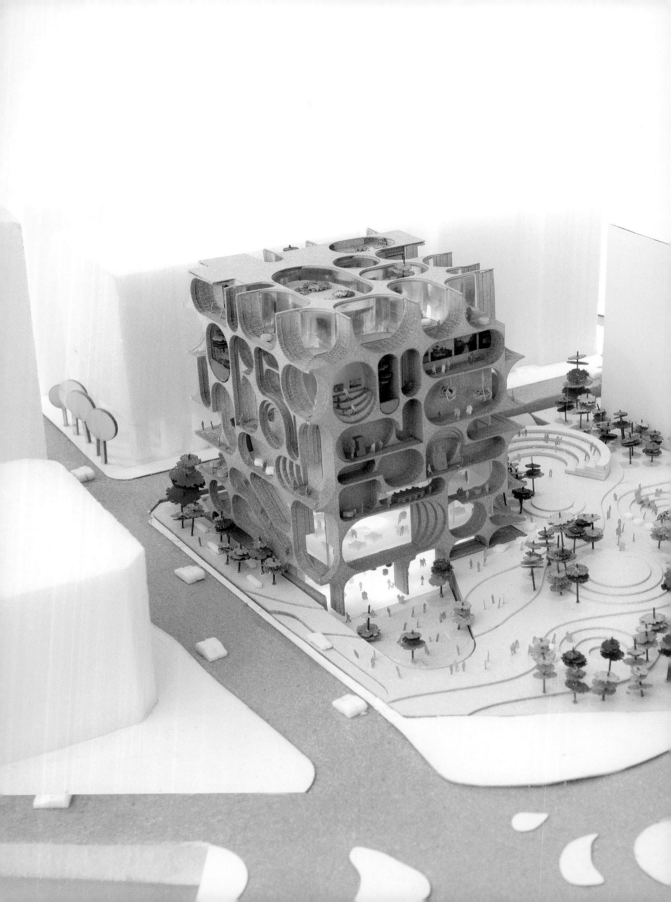

Envelope

<u>AA</u>   When we first started we were somehow dealing with either the inside or the outside in an extreme way. It was either about interiors and the small scale of the room—because that is what you get to do in New York—or the very large exterior scale of a master plan and the city. Being so focused on either the inside or the outside in that way has recently allowed us to rediscover the boundary between the two—the envelope—and reinvent it.

<u>DX</u>   The envelope is an important territory where you have to negotiate the transition between inside and outside, between what is public and what is private. It is interesting to think about the ways in which an envelope can make these distinctions less binary.

<u>AA</u>   For example, in our Miami Collage Garage project in the Design District we were interested in the thickness they gave us—only four feet—to create a vertical public space to be

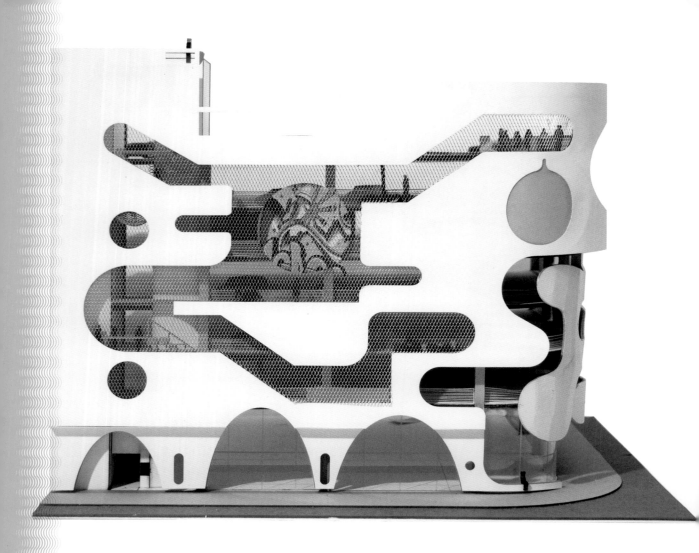

experienced in the duration between parking your car and getting to the street.

DX   What we liked is that it was a very deep program in the shallowest possible space within the shallowest type of project . . . in what some consider a shallow city.

AA   An encapsulation of the Miami scene—in a parking garage. The material is a white, perforated metal skin. Behind it everything is painted Miami pink.

DX   We've always been fascinated by the idea of a public

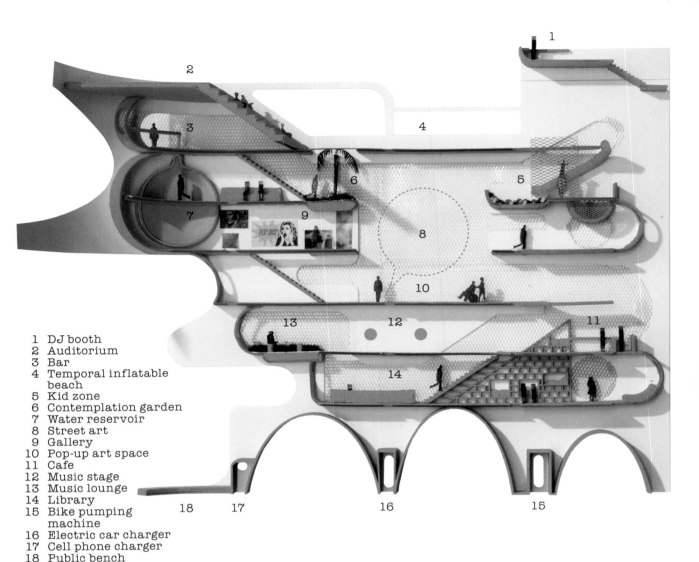

1 DJ booth
2 Auditorium
3 Bar
4 Temporal inflatable
  beach
5 Kid zone
6 Contemplation garden
7 Water reservoir
8 Street art
9 Gallery
10 Pop-up art space
11 Cafe
12 Music stage
13 Music lounge
14 Library
15 Bike pumping
   machine
16 Electric car charger
17 Cell phone charger
18 Public bench

facade. I remember going to Gehry's Disney Concert Hall when it opened and climbing up the facade. To be inside of these shapes, to discover this roof garden and for this experience to be completely public really changed the way I looked at architecture.

Envelope

<u>AA</u>   But Gehry's envelopes generally stay thin. They are just surfaces that are layered for architectural expression.

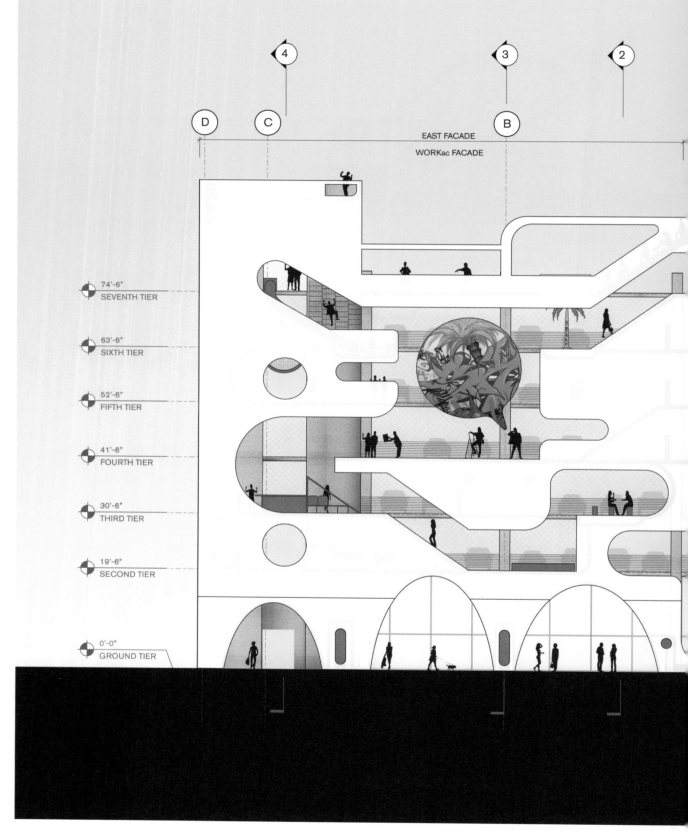

EAST FACADE

WORKac FACADE

74'-6"
SEVENTH TIER

63'-6"
SIXTH TIER

52'-6"
FIFTH TIER

41'-6"
FOURTH TIER

30'-6"
THIRD TIER

19'-6"
SECOND TIER

0'-0"
GROUND TIER

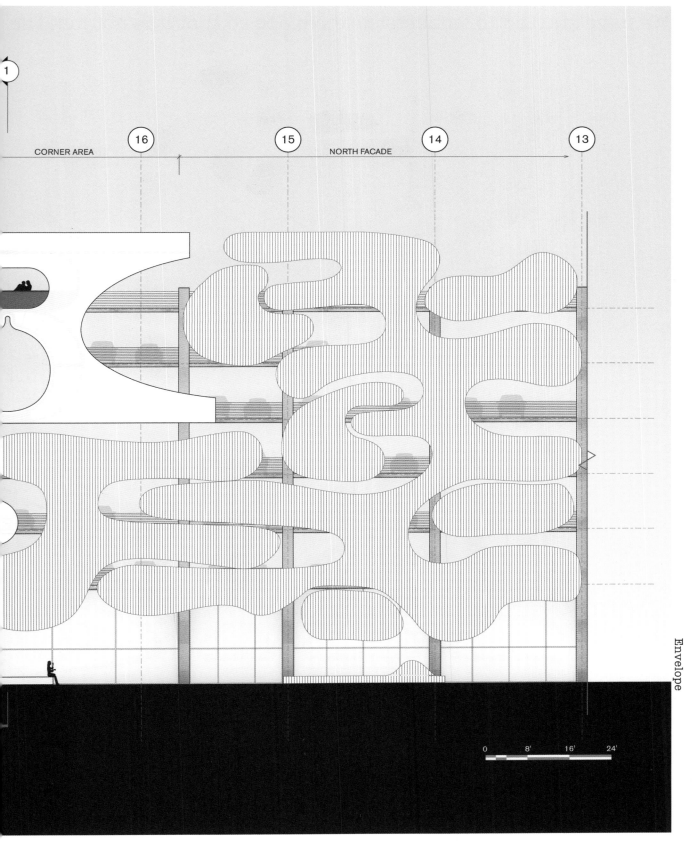

CORNER AREA

NORTH FACADE

Envelope

0   8'   16'   24'

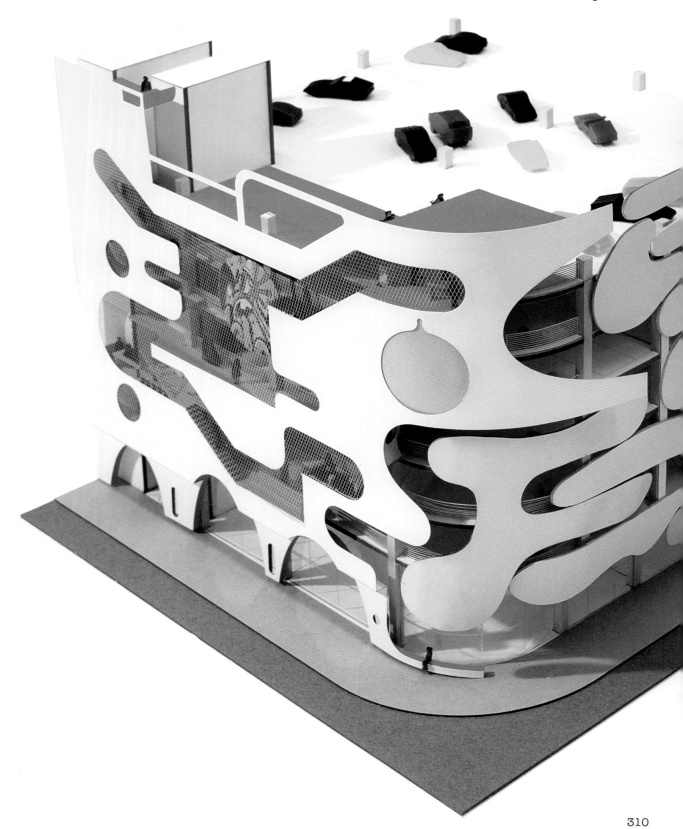

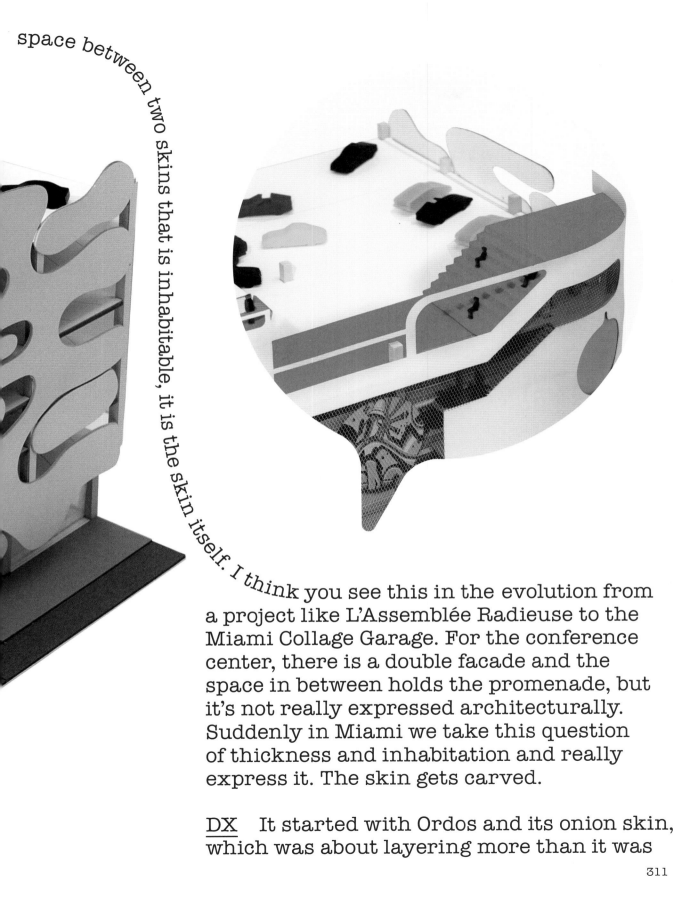

space between two skins that is inhabitable, it is the skin itself. I think you see this in the evolution from a project like L'Assemblée Radieuse to the Miami Collage Garage. For the conference center, there is a double facade and the space in between holds the promenade, but it's not really expressed architecturally. Suddenly in Miami we take this question of thickness and inhabitation and really express it. The skin gets carved.

DX It started with Ordos and its onion skin, which was about layering more than it was about thickness. Ultimately our interest in thickening the envelope stems from an ambition to add complexity, depth, and detail. In the Guggenheim Collection Center, the public cut becomes a figure that moves up the facade and provides contrast to an otherwise generic facade. That's why we don't like glass buildings that much. There is no depth, just reflection. It's very abstract.

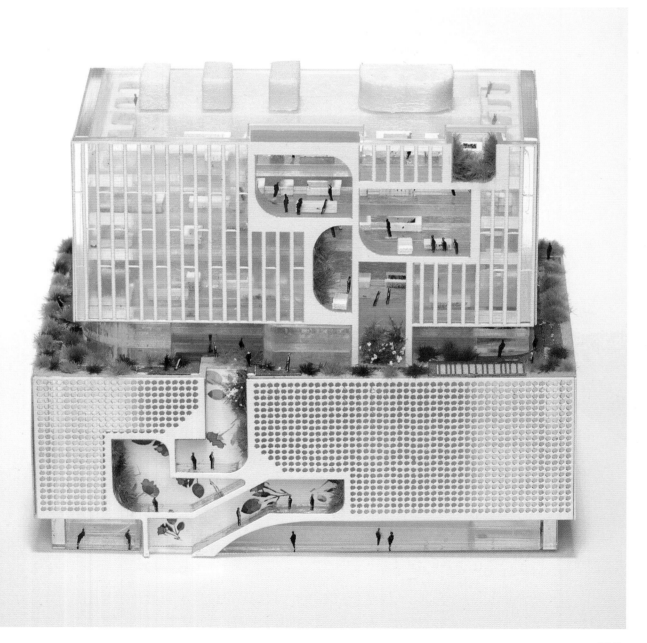

<u>AA</u>   That, and the glass facade has become *the* site of expertise in terms of technology. It has become the territory of consultants, not architects. Glass performs really well today, but we are trying to reclaim negotiations—through volume, mass, and void—that aren't just technological but are also spatial, architectural, programmatic, scalar, and material.

<u>DX</u>   The goal is to never need a consultant again?

<u>AA</u>   Funny. Transparency has also been abused to supposedly deny the distinction between inside and outside. If architecture is the drawing of boundaries then why make it invisible? We don't want to deny that boundary and the difference between inside and outside but are trying to problematize it by adding some amount of complexity. It's something we talked a lot about with Ant Farm when we were redrawing their Dolphin Embassy and designing the 3C City project: the boundaries

Envelope

314

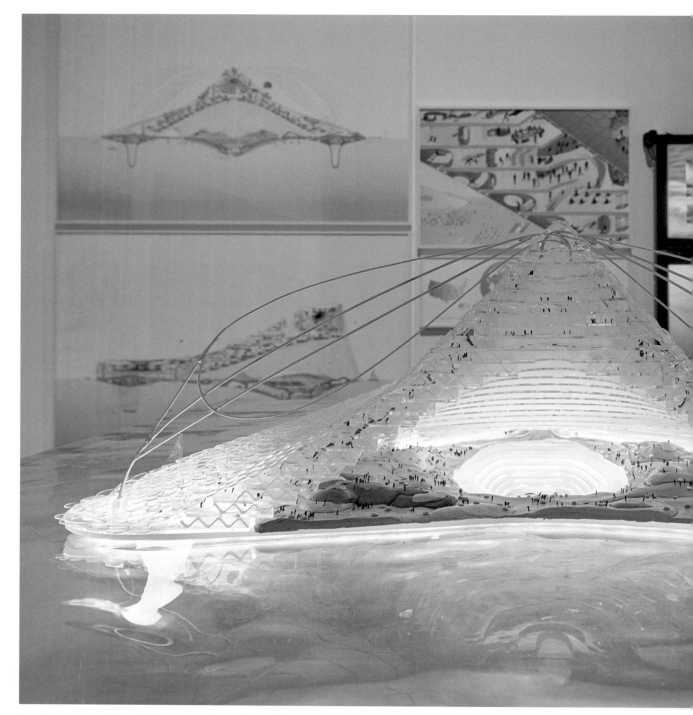

between inside and outside, water and land, people and animals, can create the space of tension and experimentation. As Alejandro Zaera-Polo writes in "The Politics of the Envelope," it may be the only thing architects have left.

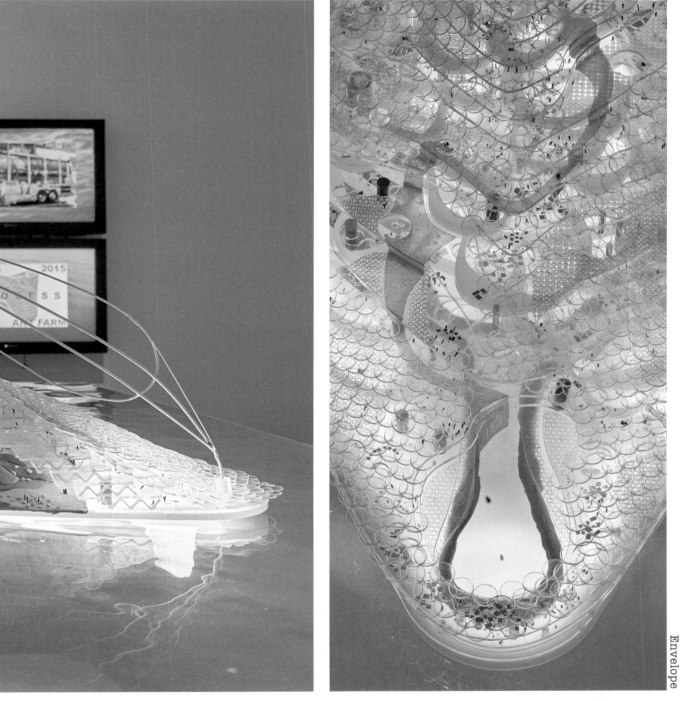

Envelope

<u>DX</u>   If all we have is the envelope we might as well stuff it with as much as we can.

318

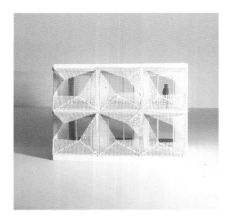
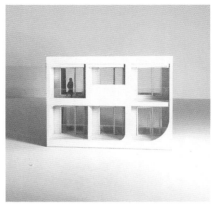

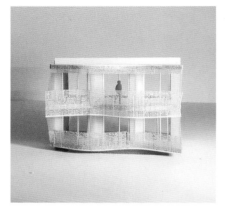

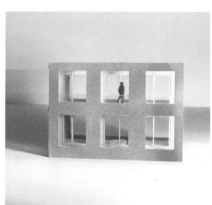
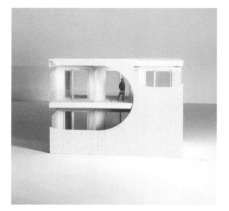

CRUISE SHIP BALCONIES

AA   The desert, in terms of the American psyche and architecture, is very powerful. We spend a lot of time in Arizona.

DX   It's such a peripheral place where you are able to free your mind and make interesting, intuitive connections. It's a real space for creativity and experimentation. We came up with the initial ideas for PF1 while on vacation there.

AA   It is definitely an inspiring environment, so much so that we decided to imagine an off-grid house for ourselves in the high desert south of Tucson, just north of Mexico.

DX   In the American Southwest architects have developed a lock on the look of the contemporary desert house—stucco ranchburger meets Frank Lloyd Wright overhangs.

AA   We wanted to channel a different, more experimental history: Arcosanti, the Biosphere . . .

DX   We've always loved the Earthship as an idea because it's a complete reinvention of how a house and its environment can coexist. The only problem is that they are buried in the ground and usually very ugly. So we liberated the Earthship, and made it fly!

AA   Without undermining the concept.

DX   Yes. Earthships use the mass of the earth as a heat sink. We simply reimagined that mass as structure that allows the Earthship to float. Not only is this mass now structural, it is also programmed, housing the bedrooms, bathroom, compositing toilet, water storage, and kitchen. During the day that section heats up and when it gets cold at night the heat is radiated back into the bedrooms. The front of the house acts in the opposite way. A greenhouse, containing a living machine for water filtration, exhausts at the very top of the roof, creating airflow and ventilation through the open living spaces. There is a north-facing terrace at the top, shaded from the south by the house itself, and below there is a shaded patio with a suspended ladder and a swing bench.

AA   Many of our ideas come together in this house, as well as many experimental references. It makes me think of Simon Ungers's T-House; the circular windows of Rem's Maison Bordeaux. At the same time, we are using adobe. There are these referential elements that come together, but there is no absolute or dogmatic quality about the design. It is all at once somehow both familiar and quirky.

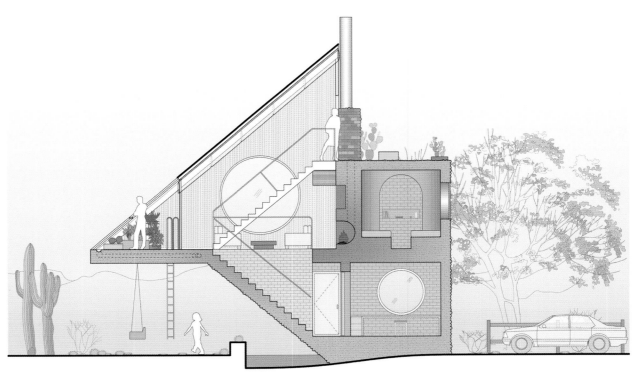

Tubac, Arizona

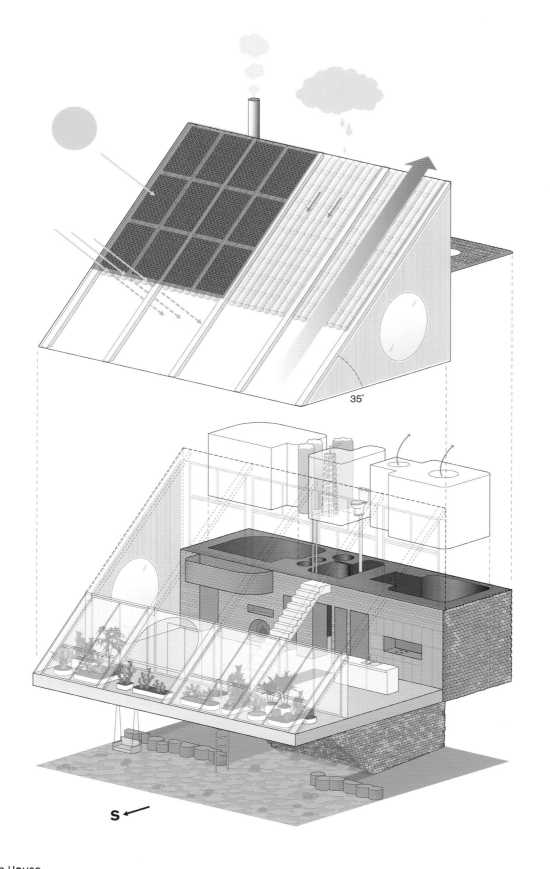

35°

S

Arizona House

Tubac, Arizona

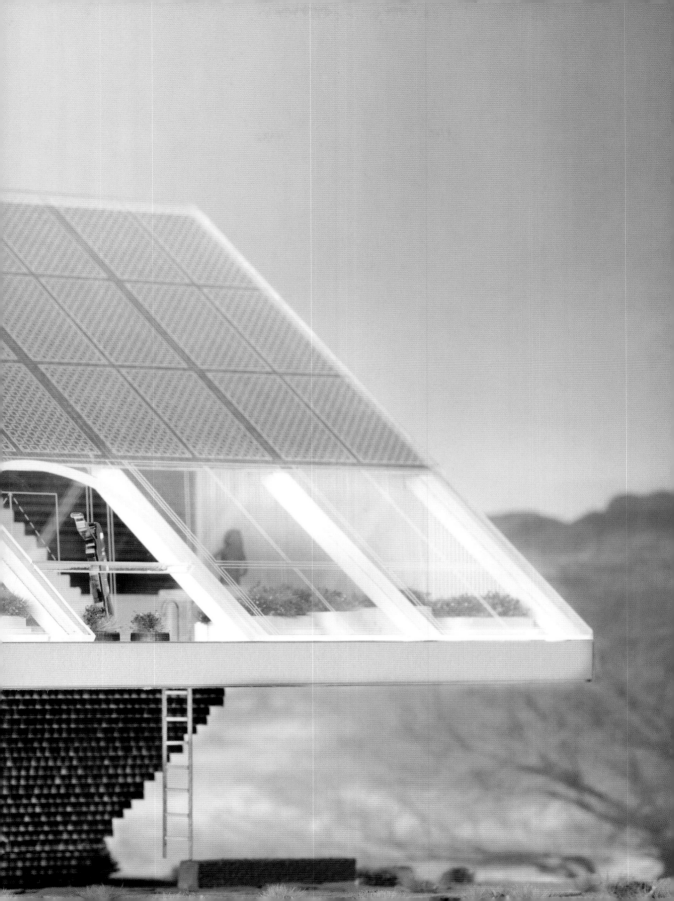

Green House

<u>AA</u>   I wonder sometimes how our interest in "green" houses relates to where we each grew up.

<u>DX</u>   I grew up in a rural place in a house that was heated by fireplace.

<u>AA</u>   [Groan] Here we go again . . .

<u>DX</u>   My bed had this eighteenth-century single-pane window above the headboard and in the morning it would be so cold, there would be frost on the inside of the window! My father would start a fire in the morning and my sister and I would run downstairs to warm up next to it.

<u>AA</u>   And I grew up in the desert where you just couldn't avoid the heat.

DX   Those memories are so strong. It's unfortunate that people think that smart houses are the future. That sort of technology would just erase these kinds of memories.

AA   It would totally homogenize any sort of climactic difference.

DX   I never liked the name *Passivhaus*—what about an "active house"? A house is so much more interesting when you have to engage it. If it gets too hot in one room, move to another. Or you can close the shades—change the actual house itself. It's architecture as clothing: if it's hot you take off your sweater; if it's cold you put it back on. They do that at Arcosanti. They change the outside depending on the

seasons, installing and removing canvas over the windows, for example. The idea that you are working with the building as part of the way that you are living in it is so much more interesting than just pushing a button that will automatically make you comfortable.

<u>AA</u>   We are not flat-out opposed to technology. It's more a refusal to turn over the agency of architecture. To have this data-driven, technologically perfect ideal of what constitutes a well-conditioned space—or a well-lit space—takes away some of its agency.

<u>DX</u>   It makes it a problem of technology and engineering and regulations rather than architecture.

<u>AA</u>   Yes. It's a cliché, but we need to push back on the technoscientific world that we are being served. There is such a long history of engagement amongst architects with questions of what constitutes the environment, but we gave it all

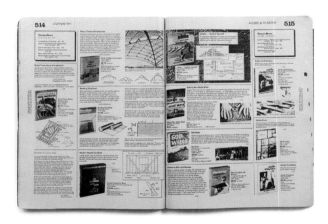

up because we just wanted to do form? And that became our expertise? That's just such a narrow understanding of architecture and what we do as architects.

<u>DX</u>   It leaves so little room to participate in the world.

<u>AA</u>   In this moment when everyone is talking about "design thinking," and "design making," we should embrace design not just as form-making but as how you hold two or more things together, that are impossible to resolve. Rather than limiting ourselves to form, why can't it be form and the environment and then some?

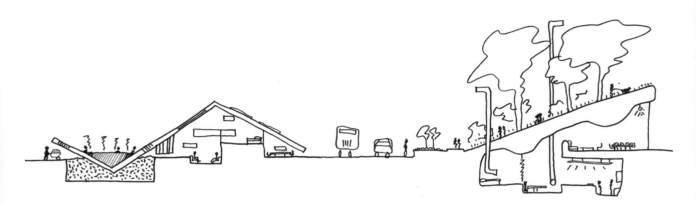

<u>DX</u>   How you resolve those differences is interesting. Sometimes it's awkward or beautiful or smooth or clunky. I think we like clunky. There is a certain aesthetic of aggregation to our buildings. Rather than being smooth, homogeneous, and resolved, the parts, forms, and systems of our projects remain legible as parts, to produce many more types of conditions and experiences.

<u>AA</u>   That's right. Why have one thing when you can have many, whether it's parts of a building or interests. I think our sense is that rather than editing out, we just need to engage as many ingredients as possible. Then the contradictions can be held together through design.

Epilogue

Kew Gardens Hills Library

Kew Gardens Hills, Queens, New York, 2008–17

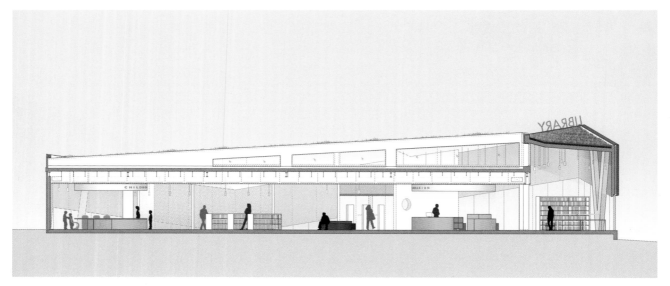

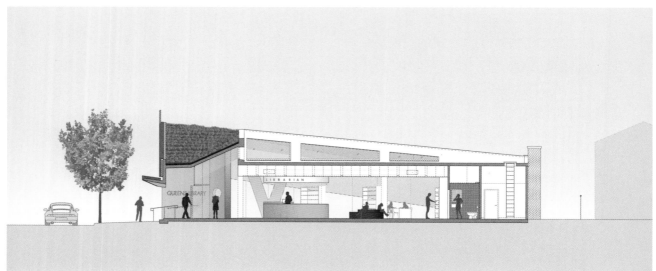

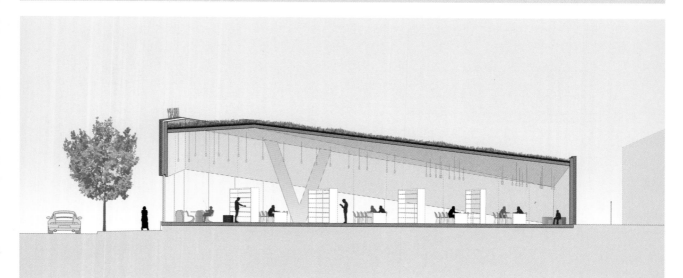

338

DX   This is a branch library in Queens that has taken forever to build. It is a little bit like a child we gave up for adoption and who has come back to us years later fully grown.

AA   Fully grown but still awkward in some ways. It's a new project that still has some old details we have now moved on from.

DX   The design phase was pretty fast, even though it required a mayoral override to allow us to build beyond legally required setbacks. The strategy was clear: to create a fifteen-foot-deep wrapper with an articulated roofscape that would expand the footprint of the existing library and enable a number of things both on the inside and for the outside.

AA   This new zone increased the floor area significantly, allowing for a series of reading rooms for different ages, and offices for librarians along the facade. On the interior, the articulated roof distinguishes those reading rooms from one another, providing privacy as the roof touches the ground for the teens and the back-of-house spaces. On the exterior, the roof bridges the smaller residential scale of the neighborhood with an institutional building that has some sense of monumentality as it lifts up at the most public corner.

DX   The articulation, sloping towards the street, also provides an opportunity for a fifth facade: a green roof that reads as a continuation of the existing garden wrapping the back sides of the library.

AA   Our wrapper really became the new public face of the library; it's much more than an addition. In fact, during construction, as often happens, most of the existing building structure was replaced. In the end it is essentially new construction.

DX   The facade holds the whole thing up. It acts like a 200-foot-long beam.

AA   The Kew Gardens Hills community has been very supportive of this project. There's something about the GFRC panels we used for the facade and the way it reads like a curtain that's being pulled up. They like the apparent weight of it all. There is a level of theatricality to it.

DX   I'm just happy people still read books and will even still need a library when it opens.

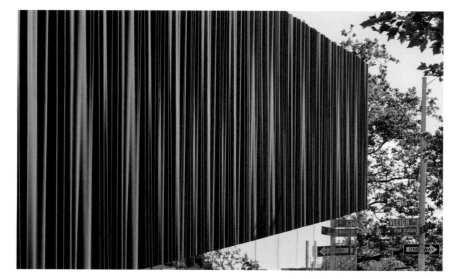

AA In an age of instant gratification, working on Kew Gardens Hills Library was definitely not instantly gratifying. In the long term, though, working with the City is quite fulfilling. You have the sense that you are working as closely to the public good as you can in the twenty-first century. I have grown to appreciate the slowness of it all somehow.

DX It wasn't always slow.

Sam Dufaux The only snag in the design process was when we had to cut the budget drastically, but it ended up making the design better.

DX Originally, we were using the bookshelves as structure—the oldest trick in the library book. When the budget crisis hit, our structural engineer, Dan Sesil, said we could just eliminate that idea because our facade

Sam Dufaux joined WORKac in 2006 and rapidly became an indispensable member of the office, becoming an Associate Principal in 2010. Sam shepherded many important projects through the design process, including Anthropologie, White Street, Wieden+Kennedy, and the Kew Garden Hills Library, bringing his Swiss sense of precision to the chaotic nature of contemporary design and construction.

was essentially already a huge concrete beam. We saved half a million dollars by making the structure cooler.

<u>AA</u> That is a rare instance of successful value engineering.

<u>DX</u> Then, it was as if we had been in a rocket ship going a million miles per hour and hit a black hole. . . . All of a sudden we were a hundred years older than everyone else.

<u>SD</u> We entered that black hole once the design had to be built. The Department of Design and Construction's Design Excellence program enlisted a sophisticated group of architects to design sophisticated public buildings. But those ambitions were lost when it came to hiring the general contractor.

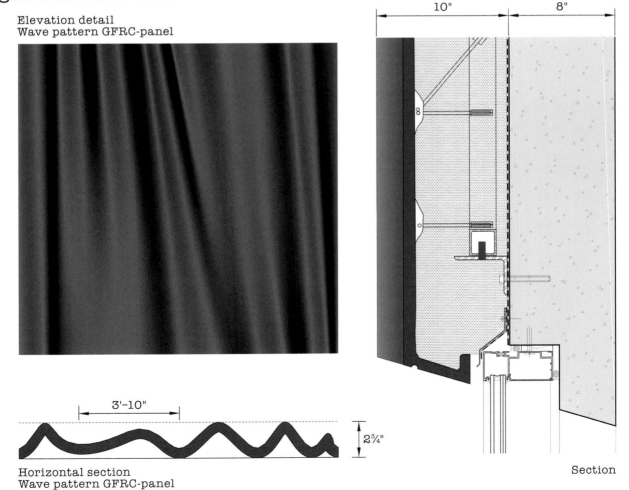

Elevation detail
Wave pattern GFRC-panel

Horizontal section
Wave pattern GFRC-panel

Section

<u>DX</u>   Ours turned out to be a scaffolding company, not an experienced building contractor.

<u>AA</u>   That was one problem. The other was that Queens Library hadn't planned around their existing library closing for the time of construction.

<u>SD</u>   They thought they would have a temporary library truck parked in front of the library while it was being built, but at the last minute they decided they needed a swing space.

<u>DX</u>   So everything was ready to go, but instead of starting the project, Queens Library had to build out their temporary space first.

<u>AA</u>   God forbid you build two libraries at the same time, or hire two contractors.

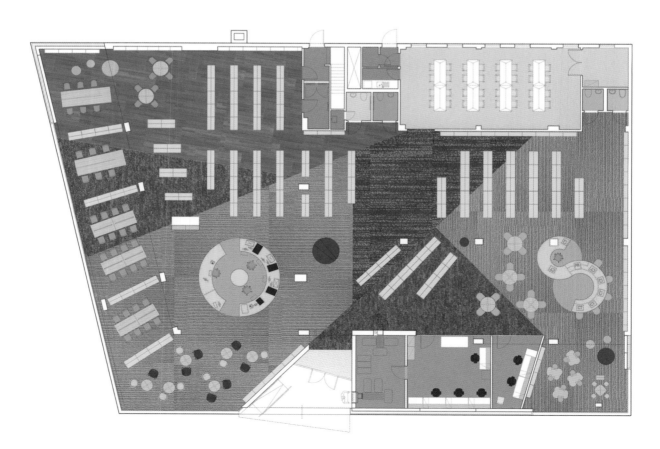

SD It took about a year and a half. That's when we realized that this contractor was a bit problematic. It was just a bunch of paint and putting books in the space.

Anyway, they finished the swing space and we were ready to re-kick off our project.

AA Only to have it delayed again!

DX The contractor brought a big trailer on site, but it blocked the whole road! They were issued a violation and everything was stopped again for a couple months. They had to build another office just for us to meet in every other week.

SD So then we re-re-kicked off the project. One of the first things we had to figure out was the exposed interior concrete. We had imagined a sort of Louis Kahn-quality.

DX But the contractor had never done concrete work before. It took them a year just to pour the foundations!

AA   And then as soon as they had finally finished the concrete—but before they had put all of the drainage lines and waterproofing along the building, they put the earth back in! They refilled everything!

SD   Just to show that the concrete was finally ready.

DX   They then had to dig all the earth back out. They later claimed they had done this on purpose.

SD   For public projects, if there is a component that requires a high level of skill you can put in a requirement for "special experience." The general contractor then needs to find someone who has done that kind of work before.

DX   It should be foolproof.

SD   But it turned out to be a shell game.

DX   The only way the GC can get around the special experience requirement is if they do the work themselves.

AA   If the foundation was any indication they were definitely not qualified to do the architectural concrete.

SD   But they did do it. We agreed they would on the condition that they work with an architectural concrete expert, Reginald Hough. We also demanded a mock-up, which, after years of refusing, the contractor finally built—and it looked pretty good!

AA   Looks can be deceiving.

SD   They started doing the actual pours and it was a disaster. Most of the time the formwork would just explode. We had these bulging concrete walls.

DX   Greg Lynn would have killed for those bulges.

SD   Except that they weren't supposed to be bulging.

DX   Anything that could go wrong, did go wrong.

AA Sam almost punched the contractor.

SD Well, for two years we were having the same meeting every two weeks. It was the exact same conversation and meeting minutes. It really messed with my head.

DX By the time the project got close to completion, much of what we had specified wasn't available anymore. The book checkout system, the highest technology in 2008, was totally defunct.

AA It's very odd to design something in 2007 and finally have it built ten years later—when you're already somewhere else in terms of your architectural investigations. It's a long time for an emerging practice that is trying to find its way. It goes to the point that you better stick to your design guns because if you're interested in consistency, architecture is unforgiving.

Acknowledgments

Alfie Koetter is the invisible third participant in this book, the listener and moderator of all these conversations. Alfie taught himself to transcribe and became a master of the foot-pedal in tireless translation from spoken to written word, then synthesized the hours of recordings and distilled the hundreds of pages of transcription to each conversation's essence.

Neil Donnelly performed magic as Alfie's graphic alter-ego, finding a way to visually transcribe fifteen years of architectural projects into spreads and compositions, looping sentences and perfectly framed paragraphs, paper stock, and spot colors. The work to create the book's aesthetic was another type of conversation, one which made us further appreciate the difficult task of adapting one design language into another.

Alan Rapp and The Monacelli Press gave us the freedom to explore, the encouragement to take risks, the support of a storied publisher and a creative, engaged editor, as well as the belief in the eternal power of a physical object in a world of digital haze.

This book has had its own five-year plan, if not longer . . . we have a folder on our server called "monograph" that dates from 2010. As such, many people collaborated with us on it over the years. Sarah Dunham helped immensely with initial research and brainstorming. John McMorrough was extremely important, flying from Michigan to New York several times to talk about our work and hammer out the broad themes and the first outline for the book's structure. Prem Krishnamurthy and Adam Michaels provided critical input and ideas early on, and Susan Sellers was an excellent sounding board at several points during the process.

Ray Adams has been one of our favorite collaborators since 2008, when he offered to shoot the making of PF1 at MoMA PS1. Ray has produced a wide range of images: work process, formal portraits, construction shots, slice-of-life documentations, and model as well as architectural photography. Elizabeth Felicella photographed all of our early work in 4×5 and we have fond memories of many long days together on site. Ari Marcopoulos, Adam Friedberg, and Iwan Baan have all lent their individual takes on our work. Bruce Damonte has created iconic images for most of our recent projects, combining special talent and a keen sense of fun, always willing to go the extra mile for one last shot.

Our current office provided much needed support to the book. Evgeniya Plotnikova has created (and re-created) drawings throughout, including for several projects that predate her time in the office. Yongsu Choung has also contributed his talents to drawings and models of our more recent projects. Kenny Petricig has visited our storage locker in Jersey City innumerable times bringing models back and forth. A former intern, Chije Kang, redrew many of our projects, creating a new consistent standard of detail, style, and color.

Maurizio Bianchi Mattioli has been an amazing collaborator and designer on many of our favorite projects, images, and designs. We were very happy to have his voice included in the book, and look forward to creating much more together. Sam Dufaux, the true hero of our Kew Gardens Hills Library story, was an essential member of WORKac nearly from the beginning and his tireless enthusiasm, dedication to design, attention to detail, dogged pursuit of perfection on site, deep knowledge of code, zoning and SCA and DDC protocol, together with his calming office presence and genuine goodness as a friend have contributed as much to the practice—and therefore this book—over the years as anyone, ourselves included. We wish him all the best in his new pursuits.

WORKers and collaborators

Architecture is a group effort and our office are our collaborators and partners in the search for new forms, spaces and experiences. We have been fortunate to work with so many people dedicated to experimentation, design, and fun. We have asked people to pull all-nighters, postpone vacations, rework drawings, and remake models destroyed in transit or, in one case, stolen by the president of Gabon. We have also had office birthday parties, drinks at the bar, drinks at the desks, and summer clambakes. Our staff has always been drawn from around the world, providing the inspiration and atmosphere that global diversity brings to a creative endeavor. We are also especially proud that so many of our "alumni" have gone on to establish exciting practices themselves.

Collaboration is at the heart of architectural practice, and we are extremely indebted to our wide group of collaborators, from both within and without the profession. These are the people who continually inspire us, and we consider these people an integral part of WORKac:

Art & Architecture
James Wines, SITE

Curation
Joseph Grima

Gardens & Community
Fritz Haeg

Branding, Advertising
Neal Arthur, Wieden+Kennedy

Civil Engineering
Jason Loiselle, Sherwood

Column Capitals, Grottos
Michael Hansmeyer

Cost Strategy
Steve Ryan, Sean Ryan, Venue

Cuisine
Michael Anthony, Gramercy Tavern, Untitled

Engineering Services, Theater
Ray Quinn, Raj Patel, Arup

Expediting, Code Manipulation, Zoning
Carlos Burbano, CCBS

Facades
Marc Simmons, Front

Farming
Michael Grady Robertson, Sawkill Farm

Hardscape/Landscape
Ken Smith

Horticulture
Don Sussman, Town and Gardens

Interactive Design
Mouna Andraos, Daily Tous Les Jours

JV Partners
Larrry Dalziel, Michael Damore, Jim Jirsa, Epstein

Landscape, Life Inspiration
Diana Balmori, Balmori Associates

Landscape Ecology
Eric Sanderson, Wildlife Conservation Society

Light Fixtures, Furniture, Design
David Weeks

Lighting
Suzan Tillotson, Tillotson Design Associates

Local Government Law, Urbanism
Gerald Frug

Mechanical, Electrical, Plumbing Engineering
Marina Solovchuk and Imtiaz Mulla, Plus Group

No Compromise Greenness
Julie Bargmann, D.I.R.T.

Preservation
Elise Quasebarth, Ward Dennis, Cas Stachelberg, Higgins & Quasebarth

Preservation, Fragrances
Jorge Otero-Pailos

Radicalism, Inflatables
Chip Lord and Curtis Schreier, Ant Farm

Soil
Paul Mankiewicz

Structural Engineering
Daniel Sesil, LERA

Structural Engineering
Nat Oppenheimer, Silman

Structure, Facades
Silvia Prandelli, Werner Sobek

Superfriends
Zhu Pei, Jeffrey Johnson & Jill Leckner, Kate Orff

Sustainability
Nico Kienzl, Atelier Ten

Textiles
Elodie Blanchard

Visionary Urbanism, *49 Cities*
Michael Webb, Yona Friedman

Project credits

21–36
White Street Loft
Tribeca, New York,
2005–10
Project team: Sam Dufaux,
Jason Anderson, Thomas
Christoffersen with
Adrienne Broadbear,
Vivian Chin, Gaustas
Eigirdas, Christo Logan,
Tamicka Marcy, Lindsey
Meyer, Amie Shao,
Dayoung Shin, Queenie
Tong, Lamare Wimberly,
Sharon Yu, Rasmus
Andersen, Younglan Tsai,
Olaf Haertel
Structural: GACE
Consulting Engineers
MEP: A&D Associates
Lighting: Tillotson Design
Associates
Textiles: Elasticco/Elodie
Blanchard
Contractor: Fred Harris
Construction
Code/expediting: CCBS
A/V: Clover Studios

37
Villa Pup
Prototype, 2003
Project team: Jens
Holm, Jeppe Kiib
Collaborators: Jim
Juvonen, writer

38
Target/Mizrahi Pop Up
Store
Rockefeller Center, New
York, 2003
Project team: Michael
Chirigos, Andrew
Galambos, Jens Holm,
Cassandra Thornburg
Collaborators: Avi
Adler, events
designers
MEP: A&D Associates
Lighting: Tillotson
Design Associates
Contractor: SRC
Industries
Code/expediting:
William Vitacco
Associates

39
Pure Form Gym
Prototype, 2005
Project team: Thomas
Christoffersen with
Mikkel Bøgh

39–43
The Good Life
Pier 40, New York, 2006
Project team: Skye
Beach, Mikkel Bøgh,
Olaf Hartel, Forrest
Jessee, Anna Kenoff,
Christo Logan,
Alex Lorimer, Ryan
Neiheiser, Dayoung
Shin, Linda Choe
Vestergaard
Collaborators: Project
Projects
Textiles: Elasticco/Elodie
Blanchard
Contractor: Eze Bongo

44
Creative Edge Parties
Greenwich Village, New
York, 2004–06
Project team: Brendan
Kelly, Judith Tse
with Ana Calle, Rune
Elsgart, Shawn
MacKinnon
Structural: LERA
MEP: A&D Associates
Lighting: Tillotson
Design Associates
Textiles: Elasticco/Elodie
Blanchard
Contractor: Eze Bongo
Code/expediting: William
Vitacco Associates

44
D'Amelio Terras Gallery
Chelsea, New York,
2005–06
Project team: Adrienne
Broadbear, Thomas
Christoffersen, Anna
Kenoff
MEP: A&D Associates
Lighting: Tillotson
Design Associates
Contractor: BKR
Development Corp.
Code/expediting: William
Vitacco Associates

45, 147
Spotwelders
Tribeca, New York,
2004–05
Project team: Gisela
Vidalle with Tina Diep,
Eckart Graeve, Cecile
Hanau, Jacob Lund
MEP: Athwal &
Associates
Lighting: Tillotson
Design Associates
Contractor: Michaels
Management &
Development
Code/expediting: William
Vitacco Associates

46
Children's Museum of
the Arts (I)
Tribeca, New York,
2008
Project team: Haviland
Argo, Mikkel Bøgh,
Katherine Eberly,
Matt Eshelman,
Anna Kenoff,
Nicholas Muraglia,
Anne Sofie Buur
Okkels, Magdalena
Szwajcowska

47
Big Love Stage Set
Dallas, Texas, 2003

48
Creative Time
Information Hub
Times Square, New
York, 2003
Project team: Rune
Elsgart, Brendan
Kelly, Jeppe Kiib,
Kirsten Krogh

49
Media Outpost
Times Square, New
York, 2004
Project team: Rune
Elsgart, Brendan
Kelly, Jeppe Kiib,
Kirsten Krogh
Collaborators: Scott
Hug, K48

50
Lee Angel
SoHo, New York,
2004–05
Project team: Ana Calle,
Benjamin Cadena,
Rune Elsgart, Brendan
Kelly, Christina
Kwak, Judith Tse,
Kirsten Krogh, Shawn
MacKinnon, Mirza
Mujezeninovic
MEP: A&D Associates
Lighting: Tillotson
Design Associates
Textiles: Elasticco/
Elodie Blanchard
Contractor: TDC
Construction, Inc.
Code/expediting:
William Vitacco
Associates

51, 243
Creative Time offices
East Village, New York,
2006–07
Project team: Anna
Kenoff with Fred
Awty, Skye Beach,
Jessica Dobkin, Olaf
Haertel, Linda Choe
Vestergaard
Lighting: Tillotson
Design Associates
Textiles: Elasticco/
Elodie Blanchard
Contractor: NJACC, Inc.

52
Stoga Stair
Hell's Kitchen, New
York, 2005–06
Project team: Adrienne
Broadbear, Olaf
Haertel
Contractor: Bogen
Construction, Inc.

53–68
Anthropologie
Dos Lagos, Corona,
California, 2005–07
Project team: Sam Dufaux,
Christo Logan, Rebecca
Satterlee with Merete
Kinnerup Andersen, Olaf
Haertel, Thomas Jensen,
Forrest Jessee, Philippe
Lacher, Elliet Spring, Linda
Choe Vestergaard
Collaborators: Ignarri
Lummis Architects,
architect of record
MEP: Polaris Consulting
Engineers
Lighting: Tillotson Design
Associates
Landscape: D.I.R.T. Studio,
Julie Bargmann
Contractor: Russel-Filand
Builders, Inc.

72–77
Ordos
Ordos, Inner Mongolia,
China, 2008
Project team: Anne
Menke with Mikkel
Bøgh, Anne Sofie Buur
Okkels, Amie Shao

78–79
El Equis
Bocas Del Toro,
Panama, 2003
Project team: Ana
Calle, Tina Diep,
Rune Elsgart, Marc
El Khouri, Brendan
Kelly, Christina Kwak,
Shawn MacKinnon,
Marc-Antoine
Maillard, Nieves
Monasterio

80–84
Cadavre Exquisse
Lebanese
Beirut, Lebanon, 2007
Project team: Merete
Kinnerup Andersen,
Fred Awty, Mikkel
Bøgh, Paul Coudamy,
Sam Dufaux, Julianne
Gola, Thomas Torslev
Jensen, Rami Abou
Khalil, Christo
Logan, Fadi Mansour,
Alex Maymind, Ana
Cristina Vargas

85–100
Public Farm 1
Long Island City, Queens,
New York, 2008
Project team: Anna Kenoff
and Haviland Argo with
Jenny Andersen, Fred
Awty, Sarah Carlisle,
Diego Chavarro, Sam
Dufaux, Katherine Eberly,
Gaustas Eigirdas, Morten
Dam Feddersen, Julia
Galeota, Alina Gorokhova,
Tamicka Marcy, Heidi
Cathrine Østergaard,
David Peterson, Melani
Pigat, Bryony Roberts,
Elliet Spring, Samuel
Stewart-Halevy, Magda
Szwajcowska, Jeffrey Yip
Structural: LERA
Textiles: Elasticco/Elodie
Blanchard
Contractor: Art Domantay
Graphic design: Project
Projects

101–102, 171–173, 214
49 Cities
Exhibited at
Storefront for Art
and Architecture,
New York; SPUR, San
Francisco; Lisbon
Triennial, Portugal,
2009
Project team: Michael
Alexander, Jenny Lie
Andersen, Willem
Boning, Sam Dufaux,
Jose Esparza, Thiago
Maso, Alexander
Maymind, Anne
Menke, Yasmin Vobis,
Hilary Zaic
Graphic design: Project
Projects

103
Locavore Fantasia
Tribeca, New York, 2008
Project team: Fred Awty

104–105
Infoodstructure
Bedford-Stuyvesant,
Brooklyn, New York,
2011
Project team: Cyril
Marsollier, Anne-
Sophie Milon

106–107
Aqualoop (1)
Shenzhen, China, 2009
Project team: Cyril
Marsollier, Mike
Robitz, Jesung Park,
Mikaël Pors

108
Aqualoop (2)
San Diego, California,
2012
Project team: Julcsi Futo

109
Flow Show
New York, New York,
2010
Project team: Cyril
Marsollier

110–112
Plug Out
Greenwich South, New
York, 2012
Project team: Dina
Braendstrup, Tobias
Herr, Anna Kenoff,
Anne Menke, Barbara
Vialette

121–137
Edible Schoolyard NYC at
P.S. 216
Gravesend, Brooklyn, New
York, 2009–13
Project team: Sam Dufaux,
Jason Anderson with Lisa
Bianchi, Michael Blancato,
Mette Blankenberg, Dina
Braendstrup, Tobias Herr,
Anna Kenoff, Cyril Marsollier,
Anne Menke, Jesung Park,
Mike Robitz, Maggie Tsang
Structural: LERA
MEP: Plus Group LLC
Lighting: Tillotson Design
Associates
Contractor: NESCO, Inc.

Edible Schoolyard NYC at
P.S. 7
East Harlem, New York,
2012–16
Project team: Sam Dufaux,
Trevor Hollyn Taub with Julcsi
Futo, Kristina Loock, Moshe
Porter, Evgeniya Plotnikova,
Maggie Tsang, Colleen Tuite
Structural & MEP:
Greenman-Pedersen, Inc.
Contractor: Skyline
Industries, Inc.

138–141
AADX Apartment
East Village, New York,
2012–15
Project team: Alfie
Koetter, Ainhoa
Martin-Sanz, Zachary
Matthews, Timo Otto
Structural: Silman
MEP: Plus Group LLC
Lighting: Tillotson
Design Associates
Textiles: Elasticco/
Elodie Blanchard
Contractor: Premier
Contracting, Jim Rice
and Roger Moore
Code/expediting: CCBS

142–143
Fifth Avenue Apartment
Upper East Side, New
York, 2005–06
Project team: Adrienne
Broadbear

144–146
Children's Museum of
the Arts (II)
Hudson Square, New
York, 2010–11
Project team: Sam
Dufaux with Lasse
Lyhne-Hansen, Nick
Hopson, Kevin Lo,
Esben Serup Jensen,
Tamicka Marcy, Beth
O'Neill, Jesung Park,
Rùni Weihe
Structural: GACE
Consulting Engineers
MEP: Plus Group LLC
Lighting: Tillotson
Design Associates
Contractor: MG &
Company
Graphic design: BASE
Design

148–149
Kate Spade Saturday
Ometesando, Tokyo,
Japan, 2012–13
Project team: Tamicka
Marcy with Ivan
Cremer, Julcsi Futo,
Ainhoa Martin-Sanz,
Victoria Meniakina
Collaborators: PLAX
Tokyo, associate
architect
Lighting: Tillotson
Design Associates

150
Creative Time in Miami
Miami Beach, Florida,
2010
Project team: Sam
Dufaux, Esben Serup
Jensen, Anders Kruse
Aagard Nielsen, Rùni
Weihe

151
Wild West Side
Hudson Yards, New
York, 2008
Project team: Mikkel
Bøgh, Bryony Roberts
Collaborators: Balmori
Associates, Fritz Haeg
Structural: LERA
Graphic design: Project
Projects

153–168
Nature-City
Keizer, Oregon
Commissioned by the
Museum of Modern Art
for Foreclosed: Rehousing
the American Dream,
2011–12
Project team: Patrick
Daurio, Marisha
Farnsworth, Joanne
Hayek, Brantley Highfill,
Allan Izzo with Colleen
Tuite, Michael Alexander,
Rubèn Carboni, Julcsi
Futo, Tamicka Marcy,
Brett Masterson, Ian
Quate, Deborah Richards,
Marcel Sonntag, Neil
Wiita, Sarah Witkin, Mei-
Iun Xue
Collaborators: Ecologist:
Eric Sanderson, Senior
Conservation Ecologist at
the Wildlife Conservation
Society, Founder and
Director, the Welikia
Project
Community and urban
theorist: Gerald E.
Frug, Louis D. Brandeis
Professor of Law,
Harvard Law School
Infrastructure: Sherwood
Design Engineers, Civil
and Environmental
Engineering
Economics: James F. Lima
Dream experts:
Wieden+Kennedy, Full
Service Integrated
Advertising Agency

169-170
Green Belt City
Las Vegas, Nevada, 2006
Project team: Sam
  Dufaux, Silvia Fuster,
  Olaf Haertel, Christo
  Logan, Rebecca
  Satterlee, Linda Choe
  Vestergaard

173-175
Pingshan Master Plan
Shenzhen, China, 2010
Project team: Anne
  Menke with Anders
  Kruse Aagaard, Sam
  Dufaux, Esben Serup
  Jensen, Rùni Weihe
Collaborators: Zhubo
  Architecture Design

176-177
Hua Qiang Bei Road
Shenzhen, China,
  2009-11
Project team: Anne
  Menke with Jason
  Anderson, Dina
  Barendstrup, Mette
  Blankenberg, Julcsi
  Futo, Tobias Herr,
  Anna Kenoff, Cyril
  Marsollier, Victoria
  Meniakina, Timo Otto,
  Colleen Tuite, Barbara
  Vialette
Collaborators: Zhubo
  Architecture Design
Structural & MEP: Arup
Landscape: Balmori
  Associates

178-179
Beijing Horticultural
Expo
Yanqing, Beijing, China,
  2014
Project team: Maurizio
  Bianchi Mattioli with
  Yuchen Guo, Kelley
  Johnson, Yifan Tao,
  Yue Zhong
Collaborators:
  Super Friends:
  Scape Landscape
  Architecture, SLAB
  Architects and Studio
  Pei-Zhu

180-183
Weifang
Weifang New Town,
  Weifang, China, 2014
Project team: Maurizio
  Bianchi Mattioli with
  Jacob Esocoff
Collaborators:
  Super Friends:
  Scape Landscape
  Architecture, SLAB
  Architects and Studio
  Pei-Zhu

184
New Silk Road Park
Xian, China, 2006
Project team: Skye
  Beach, Vivian Chin,
  Ryan Neiheiser, Linda
  Choe Vestergaard,
  Lamare Wimberly
Collaborators: Neyran
  Turan, consulting
  architect

185-208
L'Assemblée Radieuse
Libreville, Gabon, 2012-
ongoing
Project team: Brantley
  Highfill, Maurizio Bianchi
  Mattioli, Kristina Loock,
  Jack Phillips, Hyun Tek
  Yoon with Xristina
  Argyros, Bertilla
  Baudiniere, Florent Biais,
  Estelle Bordas, Ivan
  Cremer, Lucinda Eccles,
  Jeevan Farais, Julcsi Futo,
  Sarah Holland, Allison
  Hu, Kat Kovalcik, Jackie
  Krastnokutskaya, Philipp
  Kremer, Damien Magat,
  Zachary Matthews,
  Ainhoa Martin-Sanz,
  Caelin Schneider,Victoria
  Meniakina, Chris Oliver,
  Timo Otto, Quan Thai,
  Maggie Tsang, Colleen
  Tuite, Emily Wettstein
Collaborators: Epstein:
  Lawrence Dalziel, AIA,
  Cinthya Dougan, Lee
  Washesky, RA, Paul
  Sanderson, AIA, Rob
  Lopez, Steve Benesh, AIA,
  Tatjana Sofkoska, Tom
  Coronato, RA, Vincent
  Gentile, AIA
Structural: Silman
MEP: Arup
Lighting: Tillotson Design
  Associates
Landscape: WORKac with
  Mark Thomann and Island
  Planning Corporation
Facade: FRONT Inc.
Contractor: ENKA
Graphic design: MTWTF
Code/expediting: Rolf
  Jensen & Associates

210-211
Sylvan Visitor Center
Washington, DC, 2012
Project team: Maggie
  Tsang with Ivan
  Cremer, Patrick
  Daurio, Bertilla
  Martin, Seth
  McDowell, Stéphanie
  Thilleul
Collaborators: Balmori
  Associates, Alice
  Waters

212-213
UC Davis Museum
University of California
  Davis, 2013
Project team: Chris
  Oliver with Lucinda
  Eccles, Brantley
  Highfill, Alfie Koetter,
  Kat Kovalcik, Caelin
  Schneider, Maggie
  Tsang
Collaborators: Westlake
  Reed Leskosky
Structural: LERA
MEP: Westlake Reed
  Leskosky
Lighting: Westlake Reed
  Leskosky
Landscape: Ken Smith
  Landscape Architect
Contractor: Kitchell

215
Swindler Cove
Boathouse
Harlem River, New
  York, 2013
Project team: Alfie
  Koetter, Karl
  Landsteiner
Collaborators: Maria
  Cornejo, fabric
  designer; Eric
  Sanderson, ecologist;
  Rob Buchanan, rowing
  expert
Structural: Guy
  Nordenson

216
Shenda Tower
Shenzhen, China, 2010
Project team: Jason
  Anderson, Sam
  Dufaux, Kevin
  Patrick Hayes, Toon
  Kantharoup, Jaffer
  Kolb, Anne Menke,
  Benjamin Rice, Colleen
  Tuite
Collaborators: Zhubo
  Architecture Design
Structural: LERA

216
Weifang Library
Weifang New Town,
  Weifang, China, 2014
Project team: Maurizio
  Bianchi Mattioli
  with Charlene Chai,
  Jamaica Reese-Julien,
  Jenny Lin, Thiago
  Maso, Emmanuelle
  Pajot, Ioana Petkova,
  Trent Richardson,
  Felix Yang, Hyuntek
  Yoon
Structural: LERA
MEP: Westlake Reed
  Leskosky
Facade: FRONT Inc.

244
KBS+ Offices
Hudson Square, New
  York, 2015
Project team: Maurizio
  Bianchi Mattioli, Ioana
  Petkova, Sam Dufaux

225-240, 242, 244-245
Wieden+Kennedy
Hudson Square, New York,
  2011-14
Project team: Sam Dufaux,
  Tamicka Marcy, Julcsi
  Futo with Michael
  Alexander, Estelle Bordas,
  Stephanie Dennig ,Tony
  Diep, Nick Hopson, Elodie
  Le Roy, Karl Landsteiner,
  Beth O' Neill, Deborah
  Richards, Marcel Sonntag
Structural: Silman
MEP: Plus Group LLC
Lighting: Tillotson Design
  Associates
Landscape: Town and
  Gardens
Textiles: Elasticco/Elodie
  Blanchard
Code/expediting: CCBS
A/V: Diversified Systems
IT: TM Technology Partners

246, 312
Guggenheim Collection
Center
East Harlem, New York,
  2015
Project team: Trevor
  Hollyn Taub with Sam
  Dufaux, Zhao Rong,
  Karl Landsteiner

247
Metamorphosis Building
Chelsea, New York, 2016
Project team: Evgeniya
  Plotnikova with Yongsu
  Choung, Alessia
  Gilles, Samuel Saad,
  Anastasiya Vasileva
Collaborators: Mitch
  McEwen

248
Dreamquarters
Toronto, Canada, 2016
Project team: Yongsu
 Choung with Alessia
 Gilles, Samuel Saad,
 Dequan Spencer,
 Anastasiya Vasileva

249–272
Stealth Building
Tribeca, New York, 2011–16
Project team: Sam Dufaux,
 Karl Landsteiner Chris
 Oliver with Patrick
 Daurio, Timo Otto, Maggie
 Tsang
Collaborators: Michael
 Hansmeyer, artist
Structural: Silman
MEP: Plus Group LLC
Lighting: Tillotson Design
 Associates
Landscape: Town and
 Gardens
Contractor: Knightsbridge
 Properties
Code/expediting: CCBS
Preservation: CTS Group

275–278
New Holland Island
Saint Petersburg,
 Russia, 2011–12
Project team:
 Michael Alexander,
 Jason Anderson,
 Bertilla Baudiniere,
 Guilherme de Bivar,
 Estelle Bordas, Ilya
 Chistiakov, Ivan
 Cremer, Patrick
 Daurio, Tony Diep,
 Sam Dufaux,
 Julcsi Futo, Alina
 Gorokhova, Brantley
 Highfill, Nick Hopson,
 Sooran Kim, Alfie
 Koetter, Elodie Le
 Roy, Tamicka Marcy,
 Victoria Meniakina,
 Anna Menke, Chris
 Oliver, Timo Otto,
 Marta Pavao, Maggie
 Tsang, Colleen Tuite,
Collaborators: Jorge
 Otero-Pailos,
 preservationist/artist
Landscape: WORKac
Structural & MEP: Arup

279–283
Diane von Furstenberg
 Studio Headquarters
Meatpacking District,
 New York, 2004–07
Project team: Silvia
 Fuster, Eckart Graeve,
 Michael Chirigos
 with Alexandria
 Ålgård, Fred Awty,
 Benjamin Cadena,
 Tina Diep, Marc El
 Khouri, Rune Elsgart,
 Erin Hunt, Forrest
 Jesse, Brendan Kelly,
 Anna Kenoff, Martin
 Krogh, Kirsten Krogh,
 Christina Kwak,
 Martin Laursen,
 Christo Logan, Jacob
 Lund, Marc-Antoine
 Maillard, Mirza
 Mujezinovic, Dayoung
 Shin, Sylvanus Shaw,
 Andrew Sinclair, Elliet
 Spring, Dana Strasser,
 Queenie Tong, Judith
 Tse, Lamare Wimberly
Structural: GACE
 Consulting Engineers
MEP: Athwal &
 Associates
Lighting: Tillotson
 Design Associates
Landscape: Town and
 Gardens
Contractor: Americon
Code/expediting: CCBS

284–288
Blaffer Art Museum
Houston, Texas,
 2010–12
Project team: Anne
 Menke with Marta
 Pavao
Collaborators: Gensler
 Houston
Structural: Matrix
 Engineers
MEP: Shah Smith
Landscape: SCAPE
 Landscape
 Architecture
Contractor: Vaughn
 Construction

289–304
Beirut Museum of Art
Beirut, Lebanon, 2016
Project team: Maurizio
 Bianchi Mattioli with
 Mia Baraka, Nevin Blum,
 Yongsu Choung, Robert
 Boyuan Jiang, Alana
 Rogers, Thomas Smith,
 Tommaso Sordon, Easan
 Wang, Bo Zhang
Structural & MEP: Werner
 Sobeck

305–311
Miami Collage Garage
Design District, Miami,
 Florida, 2014–ongoing
Project team: Sam
 Dufaux, Hyuntek Yoon
 with Göran Eriksson,
 Yuchen Guo, Trevor
 Hollyn Taub, Yue
 Zhong
Collaborators: Terence
 Riley, master planner;
 Tim Haahs, associate
 architect

313–319
3C City
Chicago Architecture
 Biennial, Chicago,
 Illinois, 2015
Project team: Tom
 Goddeeris, Chije
 Kang with Jun Deng,
 Laetitia Fontenat,
 Margaux Guillot,
 Madeeha Merchant,
 Trevor Hollyn Taub
Collaborators: Ant
 Farm: Chip Lord and
 Curtis Schreier

321–328
Arizona House
Tubac, Arizona, 2015–
 ongoing
Project team: Evgeniya
 Plotnikova with Zuha
 Alasadi, Anna Bozek

334–352
Kew Gardens Hills
 Library
Kew Gardens Hills,
 Queens, New York,
 2008–17
Project team: Sam
 Dufaux, Anne Menke
 with Jason Anderson,
 Erica Goetz, Karl
 Landsteiner, Jesung
 Park, Evgeniya
 Plotnikova
Structural: LERA
MEP: Lilker Associates
Lighting: Tillotson
 Design Associates
Contractor: withheld
Code/expediting: CCBS

In addition we would like
to thank our amazing
administrative staff
members throughout the
years: Carolina Calderon,
Sarah Dunham, Paul
Franco, Jay Garfinkel,
Fahmidha Islam, Hannah
Johnson, Deniz Olcay,
Kenny Petricig, Jenny
Polak, Tracy Scott, and
Sofia Warren.

The following staff
members made important
contributions to WORKac
projects from 2003 until
the present that are
either still in process
or were not included in
this book: Erhard An-He
Kinzelbach, Zhehui Chang,
Kelly Colley, Tom Coronato,
Jack Cripps, Rie Davidsen,
Silvia De Lisi, Lily Feldman,
Cristina Gimenez, Cristina
Guadalupe Galván, Ben
Hauser, Anita Helfrich,
Robert Jiang, Benedikt
Joseph, Stefan Krawitz,
Phillipe Lacher, Savannah
Lamal, Radia Lamrani,
Zarifet Maqelara, Silvia
Marega, Henry Ng, Lina
Oldeen, Ericka Song,
Rayyane Tabet, Amir
Touhidi, Yixuan Wang,
Cheng Zhang, and
Joyce Zhou.

Image credits

Raymond Adams: 6, 23, 38 (top), 48, 49, 76, 77, 78 (top), 94 (top), 99, 101, 102, 103, 112 (mid.), 114 (bot.), 119 (top), 133 (top), 134, 135, 137 (bot.), 146 (bot.), 152 (top), 171, 172, 173, 187, 192–93, 194–95, 196–97, 198, 201, 202–03, 204–05, 211 (right), 214, 218, 220, 221 (top and mid.), 222 (top right), 223 (bot.), 227, 228–29, 241, 243, 251, 274, 278, 281 (bot.), 300, 301, 302–03, 307 (bot.), 312, 321, 323, 326–27, 328, 331 (mid.)

Aida Andraos: 329 (bot.)

Iwan Baan: 121, 132, 136, 137 (top), 286, 287, 288 (top), 128–29, 130–31, 284–85

David Basulto: 116 (top), 117 (bot.)

George Bellerose: 329 (left)

Alberto Bermejo Buisán: 152 (bot.)

Elodie Blanchard: 42 (bot. right)

Mikkel Bøgh: 85, 100

Bruce Damonte: 21, 26–27, 29, 30–31, 32, 33, 34, 36, 53, 55, 56–57, 58, 59, 60–61, 62, 68, 123, 124–25, 133 (bot.), 138, 139, 140 (left), 141, 222 (top left), 225, 230–31, 232, 233, 234, 235, 236–37, 238–39, 240, 249, 252, 253, 254–55, 256–57, 258–59, 260, 261, 262–63, 264–65, 266, 267, 268, 269, 271, 272, 313, 316, 317, 334–35, 336–37, 340–41, 342, 345, 346, 348, 349, 350–51, 352–53

James Ewing: 158–59, 164–65, 166, 167

Elizabeth Felicella: 28, 35, 40–41, 42 (top), 43, 44, 45, 50, 51, 52, 63, 65, 66–67, 88–89, 92–93, 94 (bot.), 96, 97, 98, 147, 279, 280, 281 (top), 282, 283

Konrad Fiedler: 87

Adam Friedberg: 142, 143

Heidi Gutman: 18

Ari Marcopoulos: 14 (top left), 38 (bot.), 144 (bot.), 145, 146 (top), 148 (bot.), 149

Taís Melillo, licensed under CC BY-SA 2.0; https://www.flickr.com/photos/tais/2587934961/: 95

Frans Parthesius: 80, 82–83

Jock Pottle: 210–11, 213, 215

Project Projects: 42 (bot. left), 117 (mid.)

Taiyo Watanabe: 64

Dan Wood: 11, 43 (bot.), 70 (top), 112 (bot.), 117 (top), 141 (bot.), 150 (top), 152 (bot.), 288 (bot.), 320 (bot.), 329 (top), 330, 331 (top and bot.), 332

WORKac: all other images

Bibliography

19: Hagberg, Eva. "On The Cusp." *Metropolis Magazine* July/August 2007. 90–91.

38: Ambasz, Emilio. *Italy: The New Domestic Landscape.* New York: The Museum of Modern Art, 1972. 280–81.

78, 171: Koolhaas, Rem and Bruce Mau. *S, M, L, XL.* New York: The Monacelli Press, 1995. 502–03, 1238–39.

101, 102, 171, 172, 173, 214: WORKac. *49 Cities.* New York: Inventory Books, 2015, 3rd Edition. Cover, 8–9, 48–49, 68–69, 88–89, 100–01.

102: Despommier, Dickson. *The Vertical Farm: Feeding the World in the 21st Century.* New York: Thomas Dunne Books, 2010. 244–45.

103: Pollan, Michael. *The Omnivore's Dilemma: A Natural History of Four Meals.* New York: The Penguin Press, 2006. 130–31.

112: MVRDV. *KM3: Excursions on Capacities.* Barcelona: Actar, 2005. 1176–77.

114: Barliant, Claire. "Urban Farmers." *Icon Magazine* February, 2012. 64–65.

115: Pogrebin, Robin. "Betting a Farm Would Work in Queens." *New York Times* 7 February, 2008. E1.

137: Von Moos, Stanislaus. *Venturi, Rauch & Scott Brown: Buildings and Projects.* New York: Rizzoli International Publications, 1987. 228–29.

146: Radice, Barbara. *Memphis: Research, Experiences, Result, Failures and Successes of New Design.* New York: Rizzoli, 1984. 14–15.

146: Pesce, Gaetano. *Les Temps des Questions.* Paris: Éditions du Centre Pompidou, 1996. 81–82.

152: Gianelli, Ida and Marcella Beccaria, ed. *Claes Oldenburg Coosje van Bruggen: Sculpture by the Way.* Milan: Skira Editore, 2006. 96–97.

211: Site. *Identity in Density.* Victoria, Australia: The Images Publishing Group, 2005. 55–56.

220: Chaban, Matt. "Columbia Names New Architecture Dean." *New York Times* 12 August, 2014. C3.

222, 223: Huber, David. "Game Changers: WORKac." *Metropolis Magazine* January, 2017. Cover, 54–55.

241: Bartolucci, Marisa and Raul Cabra. *Gaetano Pesce: Compact Design Portfolio.* San Francisco: Chronicle Books, 2003. 86–87

241: Isaacson, Walter. *Steve Jobs.* New York: Simon & Schuster, 2011. 20–21.

243: Maddock, Brent. *The Films of Jacques Tati.* Metuchen, NJ: The Scarecrow Press, 1977. 82–83.

243: *HQ: Nerve Centres of the World's Leading Brands.* Dublin: Roads Publishing, 2016. 162–63.

274: Venturi, Robert, Denise Scott Brown and Steven Izenour. *Learning from Las Vegas.* Cambridge: The MIT Press, 1972. 100–01.

281: Koolhaas, Rem. *Delirious New York.* New York: Oxford University Press, 1978. 128–29.

307: Gerace, Gloria and Garrett White, ed. *Symphony: Frank Gehry's Walt Disney Concert Hall.* New York: Harry N. Abrams, 2003. 100–01.

331: *Whole Earth Epilogue: Access to Tools.* New York: Penguin Books, 1974. 514–15.